Hiking Canyonlands and Arches National Parks

Second Edition

Bill Schneider

Published in cooperation with the National Park Service
and the Canyonlands Natural History Association

FALCONGUIDES ®

GUILFORD, CONNECTICUT
HELENA, MONTANA
AN IMPRINT OF THE GLOBE PEQUOT PRESS

FALCONGUIDES®

All interior photos by Bill Schneider.
Maps by Mapping Specialists, Ltd. © Morris Book
Publishing, LLC

ISSN 1553-2267
ISBN 978-0-7627-2540-3

Manufactured in the United States of America
Second Edition/Second Printing

To buy books in quantity for corporate use
or incentives, call **(800) 962–0973**
or e-mail **premiums@GlobePequot.com.**

The author and The Globe Pequot Press assume no liability for accidents happening to, or
injuries sustained by, readers who engage in the activities described in this book.

Contents

Arches National Park

Canyonlands National Park
Island in the Sky

Overview Map

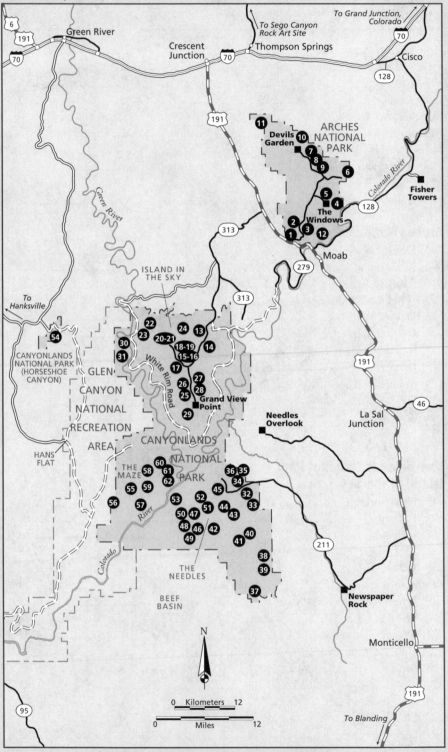

The Needles

The Maze, Orange Cliffs, and Horseshoe Canyon

Acknowledgments

This guide was a major cooperative effort between the National Park Service (NPS) staff of Canyonlands and Arches National Parks and the staff of the Canyonlands Natural History Association (CNHA). It would be most appropriate to say that it would not have happened without them.

More people helped me write this book than I can list here, but I would especially like to thank these NPS employees who helped coordinate, research, and review the original guidebook: Larry Frederick, Bruce McCabe, Mary Beth Maynard, Karen Schlom, Cary Cox, Diane Allen, and Fred Patton. Bruce McCabe and Jim Blazak helped make sure we had all updates in this revision.

Also, many thanks to CNHA employees Jean Treadway, Brad Wallis, and Gloria Brown for their help. New executive director Cindy Hardgrave also helped with this revision.

As always the staff at Falcon deserve a big thank you for putting up with my distractions while I researched and wrote the original version of this book (*Exploring Canyonlands and Arches National Parks,* 1997), with special thanks to Randall Green, our guidebook editor; Marita Martiniak, the graphic artist who laid out the book; Noelle Sullivan, the copy editor; and Tony Moore, who did the elevation charts and overview maps.

For finishing this revision, thanks to Globe Pequot staffers Scott Adams and Erin Joyce.

Preface: What is the Canyonlands?

Geographically the Canyonlands is a section of southeastern Utah, some of it embodied in two magnificent national parks, Arches and Canyonlands. But geography is only a small part of the story. Naturally the Canyonlands is much more:

- It's a rugged piñon pine growing out of solid slickrock—and the beautiful blue piñon jay screaming at you from it.
- It's the stealthy mountain lion stalking the understandably skittish mule deer, or the seldom-seen bobcat getting fat on the foolish young of the desert cottontail. You rarely see the desert cats, but they leave their story in the sand.
- It's those little whiptail and fence lizards darting away as you walk down the trail. I wonder if a scientist will ever figure out how the little lizards can run so fast on ¼-inch legs?
- It's those amazingly hardy desert plants. After being out in the Canyonlands heat a few days, you grow to really appreciate their toughness, special adaptations, and longevity. Stepping on a desert plant is like cutting down a big tree in the rain forest—except the desert plant is probably older.
- It's all that black brush everywhere, like oceans of tumbleweeds that haven't blown away yet, growing where only the hardiest plants could survive. Individual plants live for hundreds of years on almost nothing, and the desert bighorn will never have a food shortage.
- It's a whole lot of slickrock everywhere you look. Even when you aren't standing on it, you get the feeling it's only 2 or 3 inches down. As lots of names get changed and shortened as time goes by, I suspect that slickrock is really a shortened version of slick-when-wet-rock.
- It's those little potholes in the slickrock that evolve into microhabitats and then into stone-ringed "pothole gardens," like bonsai gardens where all the plants are aged but dwarfed.
- It's deep canyons winding aimlessly through the plateau and majestic arches highlighting so many skylines, with awesome sandstone spires and cliffs everywhere. And, of course, it's those "Canyonlands mushrooms," multihued, mushroom-shaped sandstone formations.
- It's the light, that wonderfully clear light. The light can change the colors of cliffs and highlight the gorgeous deep green of emerging buckthorn leaves against the reddish sandstone, especially on a rare overcast day or after a rain.
- It's the quiet. I don't know why, but canyons always seem so quiet—at least when compared to the forest, or the beach, or the prairie. Not even the wind seems to break the ever-present silence. And when there is a sound, you really

hear it. When you sneeze, it echoes for several seconds and you feel like saying, "Excuse me, Mother Nature." If you're lucky enough to get caught by an afternoon storm, you can hear the quiet burst suddenly with thunder that pounds up and down the canyon like a drum roll loud enough to shake off the desert varnish.

- It's a classroom for prehistory—ancient rock art on canyon walls and adobe ruins under sandstone overhangs left by long-gone cultures. We have to paint our houses every few years, but these cultures painted their life story on desert rocks, and it has lasted 2,000 years.

- It's getting caught in a desert rain and sitting in an alcove to watch the rocks change color and the water system start to work—little rivulets following slick-rock curves, merging, getting bigger and bigger. Those stark, dry pour overs become gorgeous waterfalls right before your eyes. The head of the newborn and very temporary stream inches its way down the dry wash. The rain washes dust off the plants; they glow a vivid green and seem to almost get up and stretch as we do at the start of a new day.

- It's the awesome flash flood that I haven't seen . . . yet. But I've seen the tracks a flash flood leaves, and I've talked to a few people fortunate enough to experience a flash flood ripping down a canyon. I'll keep coming back, hoping to see one.

Recreationally, the Canyonlands is a mecca for outdoor sports, but it's the natural wonders that make the hiking, mountain biking, four-wheeling, and river floating so great. In any geographic area, such outdoor sports are lessons in self-denial, but in the Canyonlands, they also teach self-reliance.

Perhaps most of all, however, the Canyonlands is a place to relax, take a deep breath, and let your fingernails grow. Do yourself a favor: Don't hurry through the Canyonlands. Take your time and let the nature of the Canyonlands sneak up on you and forever wrap itself around you. This can become quite a burden, however. You'll become so attached to the place, you'll have to return again and again and again.

◀ *The trails of Arches and Canyonlands National Parks often wind through gorgeous canyons such as Lost Canyon in the Needles District.*

Where to Go?

Type of Recreation	Arches	Needles	Island in the Sky	Maze	Outside Parks
Mountain Biking backcountry roads		•	•	•	•
Mountain Biking single track trails					•
Hiking short, easy hiking trails	•	•	•		
Hiking moderate hiking trails	•	•			
Hiking long hiking trails		•	•		
Hiking off-trail routes				•	
Backpacking		•	•	•	•
Vehicle Camping primitive campsites		•	•	•	•
Vehicle Camping developed campgrounds	•	•	•		•
Scenic Driving and Sightseeing paved roads	•	•	•		•
Four-Wheeling backcountry roads		•	•	•	•

NOTE: This chart is only a general guide. You can, for example, find short hiking trails in all four regions of the parks. This chart only reflects the general suitability of each area to various forms of outdoor recreation.

Introduction

The area encompassed by Arches and Canyonlands National Parks is a big place. So if you're heading for Arches and Canyonlands for the first time, where do you go?

It depends on how you like to enjoy the great outdoors. Mountain bikers, for example, might like the areas contiguous to the parks where they have more options. Ditto for four-wheel-drive fans. But here, unlike most national parks, you can also find opportunities for mountain biking and four-wheeling within park boundaries. If you're a hiker, you have lots of choices, depending on how much time you have, your physical capabilities, and how much adventure you want. For the adventure-some, it's the Maze, but for the beginner, it's Arches. For the casual tourist who wants to see some fantastic scenery without working up a sweat, it's the Island in the Sky or Arches.

The following pages of general guidelines might make planning slightly easier, but to get more details to help with your decision on where to go, refer to the overview sections in each of the major areas covered in this book—Arches National Park and the Needles, Island in the Sky, and Maze Districts of Canyonlands National Park. (The Orange Cliffs Unit of Glen Canyon National Recreation Area is included in the Maze District.) Wherever you go, however, you are not likely to be disappointed.

Planning Your Trip

Getting to Canyonlands or Arches National Parks isn't a short drive for many people. It usually takes a major effort to get there, so plan your trip wisely.

As of January 1995, along with the publication of the new backcountry management plan for Canyonlands National Park, the National Park Service (NPS) launched a reservation system for backcountry permits. You don't have to get a permit until you get to the park, but if you want the campsite you've preselected, you should use the advance reservation system. Demand for permits continues to increase, especially during spring and fall and for popular sites, so take advantage of the new system to avoid disappointment. Arches National Park is not covered by the backcountry management plan.

Before you apply for permits, digest as much information as you can about the area you plan to visit. Study the map and read whatever information you can get on the area. This saves you and the NPS time and frustration.

Getting a Backcountry Permit

Canyonlands National Park requires permits for backpacking, backcountry vehicle sites, mountain bike camping in all vehicle campsites, and day use in three areas in the Needles District (Salt Creek, Horse Canyon, and Lavender Canyon). In most cases no permit is required for day use.

The first step to getting a permit is to plan your trip. Call the park reservation office and request a backcountry trip planning guide, a free handout that will answer most of your questions. Then as far in advance of your trip as possible, request your reservations by mail or fax. If you plan a trip on the White Rim Road, you should make your reservation at least six months in advance. You can't make reservations over the phone, but you can call for assistance. All requests for advance reservations must include the following:

- Name and address of trip leader with phone numbers
- Dates and campsites or zones desired with alternatives for both
- The number of people in your group
- The number of vehicles in your group (for vehicle campers only)
- The nonrefundable permit fee

You can pay for your permit with Visa, Mastercard, or a personal check or money order made payable to Canyonlands National Park. If faxing your reservation information, use a credit card to pay. Please do not send cash. Send a detailed itinerary

Several trails in both parks go through "joints" between sandstone formations such as this one in the first part of the trail to Chesler Park in the Needles District. ▶

with alternative sites and a check, money order, or credit card information to Reservation Office, Canyonlands National Park, 2282 South West Resource Boulevard, Moab, UT 84532. Their phone number is (435) 259–4351, and their fax number is (435) 259–4285. Visit the Web site www.nps.gov/cany/ for more information.

The NPS will respond to both phone or mail requests and will send a written confirmation. This confirmation is not your permit. You must pick up your permit at the visitor center in the district where your trip begins. If you have to cancel or change your trip, please notify the reservation office as soon as possible so the campsite(s) can be made available to other park visitors.

If the campsite you want has already been reserved, the NPS will reserve an alternative site as close to your route as possible. If you send alternatives, it makes it easier for the NPS to reserve a site close to the trip you have planned. If you're already in the park, you can apply for your permit in person and pay the fee at that time. However, in some cases, the area you want to see might not have permits available, especially during peak seasons.

Fees

Fees can change from time to time, but at press time backpacking permits were $15 and backcountry vehicle or mountain biking campsite permits were $30.

Incidentally, reservation fees do not go into the general fund in Washington, DC. These fees stay in Canyonlands National Park and pay for the operation of the backcountry reservation system. Without these fees the reservation system would be impossible, and permits would be issued on a first-come, first-served basis.

Other Camping Options

If you want to stay in developed campgrounds, you can try the following campgrounds:

Devils Garden Campground, Arches National Park. This campground has fifty-two individual sites that are $10 per night and accommodate up to ten people. Up to thirty of the individual sites may be reserved through ReserveUSA.com for nights between March 1 and October 31. Reservations must be made no less than four days and no more than 240 days in advance. The remaining twenty-two campsites are available on a first-come, first-served basis each day beginning at 7:30 A.M. at the park entrance station or visitor center. To make a reservation, visit www.ReserveUSA.com, or phone the National Recreation Reservation Service (NRRS) at (877) 444–6777.

Squaw Flat Campground. In the Needles District, this campground has twenty-six sites plus three group sites and drinking water mid-March through October. There is an $8.00 per night fee. The maximum group size limit is ten people per site with the exception of the group sites.

Willow Flat Campground. In the Island in the Sky District, this campground has twelve sites, no fee, no water, and a maximum group size of ten people per site.

In a few places in Canyonlands National Park, you hike on short sections of road, such as this section of the Confluence Overlook Trail in the Needles District.

Dead Horse Point State Park. Near the Island in the Sky District, this park also has a twenty-one-site campground. You can reserve a site in advance by calling Utah State Parks at (800) 322–3770.

In peak seasons the national park campgrounds fill up fast, and spaces go on a first-come, first-served basis with the exception of the group sites, which can be reserved. The ranger on duty at the entrance station often can tell you how full a campground is. Fees are subject to change without notice.

If you can't get a backcountry permit or don't want to stay in a national park, you can often find a place on public land managed by the Bureau of Land Management (BLM) and the USDA Forest Service (USFS). There are also private campgrounds around the Needles and Moab areas. You can get information on these campsites by calling the local travel council. For more information on these camping alternatives, call the following phone numbers:

Bureau of Land Management Offices
- Moab Office (outside Island in the Sky): (435) 259–6111

- San Juan Resource Area (outside Needles): (435) 587–2141
- Hanksville Resource Area (outside the Maze): (435) 542–3461

USDA Forest Service Offices: (435) 259–7155

Travel Councils
- Grand County (Moab/Green River): (800) 635–6622
- San Juan County (Monticello/Blanding): (800) 574–4386

Where to Get Water

When you head for Arches or Canyonlands National Park, bring plenty of water with you (one gallon per person per day, stored in multiple containers). If you have to load up on water when you get to the park, you can find water at these locations:
- **Arches National Park**—Visitor center and Devils Garden Campground
- **Island in the Sky District**—Visitor center (for sale by the gallon)
- **Needles District**—Visitor center and Squaw Flat Campground
- **Maze District**—No water available

Finding Maps

Be sure to get park maps at the entrance station or from the park Web site. In addition to the park service maps, you should get more detailed maps for any backcountry excursion. For safety reasons, you need maps for finding routes and for "staying found." For nonsafety reasons, you don't want to miss out on the joy of whittling away hours staring at a topo map and wondering what it really looks like here and there.

For trips into the Canyonlands and Arches National Parks, you have two good choices for maps—U.S. Geological Survey (USGS) topo maps and Trails Illustrated maps. Well-prepared wilderness travelers take both. To find Trails Illustrated maps, check the visitor center when you get to the park, or visit gift shops and bookstores in the area. If you want a map in advance, write directly to the USGS at Map Distribution, U.S. Geological Survey, Box 25286, Federal Center, Denver, CO 80225.

For More Information

The best source of information is the NPS. In most cases you can get the information you need at the headquarters for each park, at the following addresses and phone numbers:

Arches National Park
P.O. Box 907
Moab, UT 84532
(435) 719–2299
www.nps.gov/arch

Canyonlands National Park
2282 South West Resource Boulevard
Moab, UT 84532
(435) 719–2313
www.nps.gov/cany

Canyonlands Natural History Association

Canyonlands Natural History Association (CNHA) is a not-for-profit organization that was established to assist the educational and scientific efforts of the NPS, BLM, and USFS in southeastern Utah. CNHA's goal is to enhance each visitor's appreciation of public lands by providing quality educational materials, both free and for sale in agency visitor centers. All materials have been approved after a rigorous review process managed by CNHA and the three federal agencies. Bookstore and mail order sales are CNHA's primary source of income, and proceeds support the agencies' programs in various ways.

You can help the association by purchasing items in its bookstores, making a donation, or by becoming a member. For more information on CNHA visit the Moab Information Center or any park visitor center, or contact them at Canyonlands Natural History Association, 3031 South Highway 191, Moab, UT 84532; (435) 259–6003 or (800) 840–8978; www.cnha.org.

Author's Recommendations

For People Who Want a Really Easy Day Hike

Arches	Sand Dune Arch
	Park Avenue
	Devils Garden (to Landscape Arch)
Island in the Sky	Mesa Arch
	Whale Rock
	White Rim Overlook
	Grand View
	Upheaval Dome Overlook
Needles	Pothole Point
	Cave Spring
Maze	Colorado/Green River Overlook (to Beehive Arch)

For People Who Want an Easy But Not Too Easy Day Hike

Arches	Broken Arch
	Tower Arch
Island in the Sky	Murphy Point
	Fort Bottom (access by four-wheel-drive)
Needles	Slickrock Foot Trail
	The Joint Trail
Maze	The Granary

For People Who Want a Moderately Difficult Hike

Arches	Devils Garden (to Double O Arch)
	Delicate Arch
	Fiery Furnace
Island in the Sky	Neck Spring
	Lathrop (to canyon rim)
	Moses (access by four-wheel-drive)
Needles	Squaw Canyon/Big Spring Canyon
	Chesler Park Loop
	Devils Pocket Loop

Maze	The Great Gallery
	Maze Overlook
	Colorado/Green River Overlook
	Spanish Bottom

For People Who Want a Long, Hard Day Hike

Arches	Devils Garden (primitive loop)
Island in the Sky	Syncline Loop
	Murphy Basin
	Alcove Spring
Needles	Lost Canyon
	Squaw Canyon/Elephant Canyon
	Druid Arch
	Confluence Overlook
	Upper Salt Creek
Maze	Harvest Scene

For That First Night in the Wilderness

Island in the Sky	Murphy Point
	Upheaval Canyon
Needles	Upper Salt Creek (out-and-back option)
	Squaw Canyon/Big Spring Canyon
	Elephant Hill to Squaw Canyon
	Chesler Park Loop
Maze	Happy Canyon
	Colorado/Green River Overlook

For Photographers

Arches	Devils Garden
	Park Avenue
	Fiery Furnace
	Delicate Arch
Island in the Sky	Murphy Point
	Moses (access by four-wheel-drive)
	White Rim Overlook
	Grand View

Needles	The Joint Trail
	Peekaboo
	Lost Canyon
	Confluence Overlook
	Devils Pocket Loop
Maze	Maze Overlook
	Harvest Scene
	Colorado/Green River Overlook

For People Who Want a Multiday Backcountry Adventure

Island in the Sky	Alcove Spring/Syncline Loop
Needles	The Big Needles Loop
	Chesler Park/Devils Kitchen
	Upper Salt Creek
Maze	Harvest Scene

For Trail Runners and Power Hikers

Island in the Sky	Neck Spring
	Lathrop (to canyon rim)
	Upheaval Canyon
Needles	Squaw Canyon/Big Spring Canyon
	Squaw Canyon/Elephant Canyon

Hikes Rated by Difficulty

Easy Hikes

Hike 1: Desert Nature Trail
Hike 2: Park Avenue
Hike 3: Balanced Rock
Hike 4: Windows Primitive Loop
Hike 5: Double Arch
Hike 7: Sand Dune Arch
Hike 8: Broken Arch
Hike 9: Skyline Arch
Hike 10: Devils Garden (to Landscape Arch)
Hike 14: Lathrop (to rim)
Hike 15: Mesa Arch
Hike 26: Murphy Point
Hike 28: White Rim Overlook
Hike 29: Grand View
Hike 32: Roadside Ruin
Hike 33: Cave Spring
Hike 34: Pothole Point
Hike 35: Slickrock Foot Trail
Hike 38: Castle Arch
Hike 39: Fortress Arch

Moderate Hikes

Hike 6: Delicate Arch
Hike 10: Devils Garden (to Double O Arch)
Hike 11: Tower Arch
Hike 13: Neck Spring
Hike 14: Lathrop (to White Rim Road)
Hike 16: Aztec Butte
Hike 19: Whale Rock
Hike 21: Upheaval Dome Overlook
Hike 22: Upheaval Canyon
Hike 23: Moses
Hike 30: Fort Bottom
Hike 43: Squaw Canyon/Big Spring Canyon
Hike 45: Elephant Hill to Squaw Flat
Hike 46: Druid Arch
Hike 48: The Joint Trail
Hike 49: Druid Arch West
Hike 50: Chesler Park Loop
Hike 51: Devils Pocket Loop

Difficult Hikes

Hike 10: Devils Garden
Hike 14: Lathrop (to Colorado River)
Hike 17: Wilhite
Hike 18: Alcove Spring
Hike 20: Syncline Loop
Hike 22: Upheaval Canyon
Hike 25: Murphy Basin
Hike 27: Gooseberry
Hike 36: Confluence Overlook
Hike 37: Upper Salt Creek
Hike 40: Peekaboo
Hike 41: Lost Canyon
Hike 44: Big Spring Canyon/Elephant Canyon
Hike 53: Lower Red Lake

Multiday Hikes

Hike 14: Lathrop (to Colorado River)
Hike 17: Wilhite
Hike 18: Alcove Spring
Hike 20: Syncline Loop
Hike 22: Upheaval Canyon
Hike 24: Alcove Spring/Syncline Loop
Hike 25: Murphy Basin
Hike 27: Gooseberry
Hike 37: Upper Salt Creek
Hike 40: Peekaboo
Hike 41: Lost Canyon
Hike 42: Lost Canyon/Elephant Canyon
Hike 43: Squaw Canyon/Big Spring Canyon
Hike 44: Big Spring Canyon/Elephant Canyon
Hike 46: Druid Arch
Hike 47: Chesler Park/Devils Kitchen
Hike 49: Druid Arch West
Hike 50: Chesler Park Loop
Hike 51: Devils Pocket Loop
Hike 52: The Big Needles Loop
Hike 53: Lower Red Lake

How to Use This Guide

This guide won't answer all the questions you have concerning your trip to Arches or Canyonlands National Parks, but it should answer most of them. This book provides most of the basic information you need to plan a successful trip.

Distances

In this guide, most distances came from odometer readings or from NPS signs and brochures. However in some cases, estimates were made. Keep in mind that distance is often less important than difficulty. A rocky, 2-mile uphill trail can take longer and require more effort than 4 miles on a well-contoured trail on flat terrain. Often the trails and roads of these parks are better measured in hours instead of miles.

Ratings

Difficulty ratings for trails serve as a general guide only, not the final word. What is difficult to one hiker may be easy to the next. In this guide difficulty ratings consider both how long and how strenuous the route is. Here are general definitions of the ratings:

Easy: Suitable for any hiker, including small children, without serious elevation gain, hazardous sections, or places where the trail is hard to follow.

Moderate: Suitable for hikers who have some experience and at least an average fitness level. Probably not suitable for small children. The hike may have some short sections where the trail is difficult to follow and often includes some hills.

Strenuous: Suitable for experienced hikers at an above-average fitness level, often with sections that are difficult to follow or some off-trail sections that could require knowledge of route-finding with topo map and compass, sometimes with serious elevation gain, and possibly some hazardous conditions.

Roads

In the back of this book you'll find an Appendix on backcountry roads. To help you plan your trip, each road description in this section includes vehicle recommendations. Vehicle ratings for backcountry roads came from experience in driving the roads and from NPS recommendations. These recommendations are, admittedly, on the conservative side. Play it safe, take a high-clearance four-wheel-drive vehicle to safely cover any road in the park. A high-clearance four-wheel-drive vehicle is required for all backcountry roads in the Needles and the Maze.

Key to Unpaved Roads in Canyonlands and Arches National Parks

	2WD-LC	2WD-HC	4WD-LC	4WD-HC
Arches	Salt Valley		Willow Flats	Four-Wheel-Drive Road
Island in the Sky	Green River Overlook			Shafer Trail, Taylor Canyon, White Rim Road, Lathrop Canyon
Needles	Cave Spring	Elephant Hill (to the trailhead)		Colorado Overlook, Salt Creek, Horse Canyon, Lavender Canyon, Elephant Hill, Devils Lane
Maze		Horsehoe Canyon, Gordon Flats, Waterhole Flat, Hite		Dollhouse, Millard Canyon, Maze Overlook, North Point, Panorama Point, Cleopatra's Chair, Big Ridge, Sunset Pass, Golden Stairs

NOTE: 2WD (two-wheel-drive); 4WD (four-wheel-drive); HC (high clearance); LC (low clearance)

*Many trails in Canyonlands National Park
are rough and marked only with cairns.*

Hypsometry

The larger scale maps in this book use hypsometry, or elevation tints, to portray relief. Each gray tone represents a range of equal elevation. This portrayal of relief uses relatively large contour intervals, so it only gives the reader a rough idea of elevation gain and loss. The darker tones are lower elevations and the lighter grays show areas of higher altitude. Density or proximity of contour lines or narrow bands of tints indicate steep terrain, whereas larger distances between contour tints show areas of more gradual slope.

Types of Trips

Suggested hikes have been split into the following categories:

Loop: Starts and finishes at the same trailhead, with no (or very little) retracing of your steps.

Shuttle: A point-to-point trip that requires two vehicles (one left at the other end of the trail) or an arrangement where hikers are picked up at a designated time and place. The best way to manage the logistical problems of shuttles is to arrange for another party to start at the other end of the trail. When the two parties meet at a predetermined point, they trade keys. When finished, they drive each other's vehicle home.

Out-and-Back: Traveling to a specific destination, then retracing your steps back to the trailhead.

Managing the Backcountry

In January 1995, after extensive public input, the NPS published a new backcountry management plan for Canyonlands National Park. The new plan was needed because visitation had quadrupled from 1984 (105,646 visitors) to 1993 (434,844), and this increased use posed many threats to the finite resources of the park. The plan established new regulations to preserve the fragile high desert environment.

The 1995 plan, which does not cover Arches National Park:

- established nineteen backcountry zones for backpacking. Only three—Island in the Sky/Syncline, Needles/Upper Salt Creek and Needles/Needles Trails—have designated campsites. The remaining zones allow at-large camping.
- limited the total number of backcountry permits to sixty-three.
- established a backcountry permit reservation system.
- established a user fee to fund the backcountry reservation system and maintain backcountry facilities.
- limited the length of backcountry stays to seven to ten days in any zone and established a limit of fourteen consecutive days per trip.
- limited backpacking group size to seven per party in the Needles and Island in the Sky, and five per party in the Maze.
- established vehicle group size at ten for the Needles, fifteen for Island in the Sky, and nine for the Maze.
- closed two sensitive areas to all entry.
- prohibited all wood fires and wood gathering throughout the backcountry.
- closed sections of some roads by converting them to hiking trails.
- removed all garbage cans from the backcountry.
- established acceptable noise levels.
- prohibited all pets in the backcountry.
- limited stock use (horses, mules, and burros) of the backcountry and prohibited llamas and goats.
- required use of pelletized feed for stock forty-eight hours before and during any trip to the backcountry.
- allowed caches under some circumstances.

Special Regulations for Backcountry Use

Canyonlands and Arches National Parks have strict regulations to protect the fragile environment. Under these regulations, you may not:

- take pets, with or without a leash, into the backcountry.
- drive vehicles off established roads.

- collect, destroy, or deface any mineral, plant, wildlife, or natural feature.
- take firearms or any implement designed to discharge missiles into the backcountry.
- swim or bathe in any water source with the exception of the Colorado and Green Rivers and along the Salt Creek backcountry road.
- have a wood fire or gather wood.
- go into the backcountry without an overnight permit. (See page 2 for information on obtaining permits.)

What is At-Large Backpacking?

In many areas in Canyonlands National Park—such as Lavender Canyon and Lower Salt Creek in the Needles District, below the White Rim Road in the Island in the Sky District and most of the Maze District—the NPS allows what is called "at-large" backpacking. All vehicle camping in these areas is restricted to designated backcountry camps, but backpackers can choose their own low-impact sites. However, you must follow the regulations listed below and camp at least 1 mile from and out-of-sight of any road or trailhead. This does not mean you can drive partway up a backcountry road, stop at a convenient point, then carry your pack a mile away from the road and spend the night. You must park your vehicle at a trailhead, not along the road.

The only place you can leave your vehicle overnight is at an official vehicle camp (if you have a permit for that site) or at a trailhead for either a road or a trail. For example, you can at-large backpack in Lavender Canyon or Salt Creek in the Needles, but you must leave your vehicle at the locked gate for these areas.

In Arches National Park, backpacking is allowed 0.5 mile from trails and 1 mile from roads with a few other restrictions.

Most backpacking permits in the three districts of Canyonlands National Park (but not in Arches National Park) are for at-large campsites. This means you can camp anywhere subject to the following regulations. All at-large campsites must be:

- 300 feet from any water source, including seeps, potholes, springs, and streams, not including the Green and Colorado Rivers.
- 300 feet from any archaeological site, including alcoves, rock art, surface scatters of lithics or ceramics, and partial or complete structures or ruins.
- at least 1 mile from a trailhead or road, including backcountry roads.
- within the zone for which the permit is issued.
- in an area open to at-large camping.
- left with the least possible evidence of use and environmental impact.

- accessed by the least impacting route, using washes or rock surfaces to reach the campsite.
- located on rock surfaces, previously disturbed sites, or surfaces without cryptobiotic soil crusts or vegetation.

Backpacking Permits By Zone

Area	Zone Name	Number of Permits
Island in the Sky	Taylor Canyon	4
	Syncline	1★
	Upper West Basins	3
	Lower Basins	2
	Gooseberry/Lathrop	2
	Murphy Point	1
Needles	Davis and Lavender	2
	Upper Salt Creek	4★
	Salt Creek/Horse Canyon	4
	Butler/West Side Canyons	2
	Red Lake/Grabens	5
	Needles North	1
Maze	Maze Area	11
	Orange Cliffs	1
	High Spur	3

★ Designated backcountry campsites

For detailed backcountry camping information, visit the official Canyonlands National Park Web site at www.nps.gov/cany. For excellent maps of the backcountry zones, visit www.nps.gov/cany/maps.

Hiking the High Desert

The Canyonlands are high desert country, so prepare yourself for the climate. Have the right equipment and clothing, and be mentally prepared.

For starters, make one major attitude adjustment: In most cases, the only water you'll ever drink in the desert is the water you carry with you. This differs significantly from most hiking areas, where you can bank on filtering or purifying water from a stream or lake along the way. This is actually a difficult adjustment for people accustomed to hiking in nondesert climates, especially if it's their first time in the high desert. It won't be long, however, before the special character of the canyons creeps into your body and takes root. Then you'll love the place, no matter how dry it is.

When to Hike

In northern climates, most hiking occurs during the summer months, particularly July and August. But summer might be the worst time to go to Canyonlands. Instead, choose one of the "shoulder seasons"—spring (March, April, or May), when the fabulous desert wildflowers bloom, or in the fall (September, October, or November), when the weather is more pleasant. Spring and fall temperatures usually drop to a level that makes hiking much more enjoyable than in summer.

To get extra enjoyment out of hiking the high desert, take advantage of the early morning or late evening. The desert light is the purest early and late in the day, when the temperature usually drops to a more tolerable level. Plus, you stand a better chance of seeing desert wildlife at these times. Some desert fauna is nocturnal, and even diurnal species often remain inactive during midday but come out at dawn and dusk.

The Water Dilemma

Hiking in the high desert, simply put, provides more exercise than hiking in moist climates. You really can't go lightweight, because you need to carry water. Experts recommend taking one gallon of water per person per day for long day hikes and even more for backpacking. For many people this essentially limits the length of their trip to two or three nights. A gallon of water weighs about eight pounds. That means, for example, that a four-person group on a three-day trip (two nights out) would have to carry a total of ninety-six pounds of water.

If you're planning a longer trip and the weight of your pack is stretching your physical abilities, reduce your load, but do not reduce your water supply. For example, abandon optional equipment such as extra camera gear or clothing, or at least invest in lightweight gear. You will live if you have to wear the same underwear two days in a row, but running short on water can kill you. It might be tempting to leave

Some trails simply follow the path of least resistance, which is often a dry wash. It might not be the shortest distance between two points, but it helps minimize damage to the cryptobiotic crust.

your tent home to save weight, but a tent can be a lifesaver if bad weather blows in. However, you can take a lightweight, three-season tent, or a four-person group can use a lightweight four-person tent instead of two smaller tents, which together weigh more.

Food presents a special challenge. The lightest food (pre-made, freeze-dried meals or dehydrated foods such as pasta, rice, and oatmeal) take water to prepare. This means you have to use precious water for cooking. This might seem like heresy to backpacking gourmands, but one alternative is to take the no-cooking option. Prepare evening meals in advance in leak-proof containers or make sandwiches. Plan on snacking for breakfast and lunch. This might seem radical, but you save weight in two ways: You use less water and need less gas for your stove. You could, actually, leave your stove and gas at home if you're sure of the weather forecast and have no chance of running into cold weather.

The Desert Sun

Although lack of water presents the biggest challenge for hikers, the abundance of sunshine also requires special preparation and planning. Three pieces of equipment that might be optional elsewhere—a wide-brimmed hat, sunglasses, and sunscreen—are essential for desert hiking.

Don't underestimate the power of the desert sun. You might think you have a tan and don't need sunscreen, but you're almost always wrong. If you're still lily white from your winter hibernation, start hiking with sunscreen protection rated SPF 25 to 30. Later, if you want a tan, move down to SPF 8 to 12. If you expose your skin without sunscreen, do it for only an hour or so per day. You'll be unpleasantly shocked by how fast you can burn, and a bad sunburn besides being unhealthy can ruin your vacation.

Also pay attention to the type of clothing you wear. When choosing your wardrobe, go "light and white" and use natural fibers such as cotton whenever possible. A round, wide-brimmed hat with a drawstring keeps more sun off your neck and ears than a baseball hat, and will stay on. If the wind keeps blowing off your hat, you might not wear it and will get fried by the desert sun. In addition, that old standby, the bandanna, can be draped from the back of your hat to prevent you from becoming a "redneck." Long pants and long-sleeve shirts reduce the amount of skin exposed to the sun. The sun isn't the only reason to wear long pants, however. If you're going cross-country or on a rough trail, you should definitely wear long pants. If you don't, the desert flora (most species armed with spines) will constantly take little nicks out of your legs. Such wounds will heal, of course, but wearing long pants will be less painful.

Another piece of equipment essential for enjoying the desert is good footwear. You don't need the extra-heavy boots mountain climbers wear, but you need sturdy boots of at least ankle height. Running or cross-training shoes might suffice for easier trips on well-defined trails, but anything long and rough calls for sturdier boots, even more so than in forested hiking areas in temperate-zone mountain ranges.

Faint Trails

Most of the short, frequently used trails in Arches and Canyonlands National Parks are well defined and marked, and few people have problems following them. However, some trails receive infrequent use and can be difficult to find in places. Plus, terrain such as slickrock and canyon washes makes construction and maintenance of permanent trails difficult.

If you get in a situation where you can't see the trail, don't panic. Usually you can look ahead to see where the trail goes. Even if you can't, don't worry about being off the trail for a short distance. Some trails simply follow canyon washes with an occasional cairn to remind you that you're still on the correct route. In a narrow canyon, the trail can rarely go anywhere but between the canyon walls. However, if you've gone a long way without seeing a cairn, you might be in the wrong canyon and need to backtrack to the last cairn. Again, don't panic. Get out the topo map and

Many trails simply follow the canyon wash.

figure out where you went wrong. Better yet, keep it out at all times, so you'll always know your exact location.

Most trails in these parks are marked with cairns, but cairns can be knocked down or blown away. Also, hikers have been known to put up "unofficial" cairns to mark a route back to their camp or favorite hiking area.

Sharing

Each of us wants our own private wilderness area, but that only happens in our dreams. Many people use the national parks. To give everybody an equal chance at a great experience, all of us must work at politely sharing the wilderness. In some places in Canyonlands, for example, hikers, mountain bikers, and four-wheelers share the same backcountry road. Every situation is different, but safety and courtesy should always dictate who yields. In most cases, hikers should yield to mountain bikers or vehicles, and mountain bikers should yield to vehicles.

In some cases, hikers share trails with backcountry horsemen (although stock use is infrequent at Canyonlands and Arches because of the dry climate). Both hikers and backcountry horsemen have every right to be on the trail. Keep in mind that horses and other stock animals are much less maneuverable than hikers, so it becomes the hiker's responsibility to yield the right-of-way. Hike uphill from the trail about 20 feet and stand quietly while stock passes.

Choosing a campsite also requires the polite sharing of wilderness. If you get to a popular at-large camping area late in the day and all good campsites are taken, don't crowd another camper. These sites rightfully go on a first-come, first-served basis. If you're late, you have the responsibility to move on or take a less desirable site a respectable distance away from other campers. In some backcountry zones, designated campsites have multiple tent sites. Try to pick one as far away from other campers as possible.

Zero Impact

Going into a national park such as Yellowstone is like visiting a famous museum. You obviously do not want to leave your mark on an art treasure in the museum. If everybody going through the museum left one little mark, the piece of art would be quickly destroyed—and of what value is a big building full of trashed art? The same goes for a pristine wilderness such as Canyonlands and Arches National Parks, which are as magnificent as any masterpiece by any artist. If we all left just one little mark on the landscape, the wilderness would soon be despoiled.

A wilderness can accommodate a reasonable amount of human use as long as everybody behaves. But a few thoughtless or uninformed visitors can ruin it for everybody who follows. The need for good manners applies to all wilderness users, not just backpackers. Day hikers should also strictly adhere to the "zero-impact" principles. We all must leave no clues that we have gone before.

Most of us know better than to litter—in or out of the wilderness. Be sure you leave nothing, regardless of how small it is, along the trail or at the campsite. This means you should pack out everything, including orange peels, flip tops, cigarette butts, and gum wrappers. Also, pick up any trash that others leave behind.

Follow the main trail. Avoid cutting switchbacks and walking on vegetation beside the trail. In the desert, some terrain is very fragile so, if possible, stay on the trail. If you're hiking off-trail, try to hike on slickrock or in canyon washes.

Don't pick up "souvenirs," such as rocks, antlers, or wildflowers. The next person wants to see them, too, and collecting such souvenirs violates park regulations.

Avoid making loud noises that may disturb others. Remember, sound travels easily to the other side of the canyon. Be courteous.

Bury human waste 6 to 8 inches deep and pack out used toilet paper. This is a good reason to carry a lightweight trowel. Keep wastes at least 300 feet away from any water source.

Finally, and perhaps most importantly, strictly follow the pack-in/pack-out rule. If you carry something into the backcountry, consume it or carry it out.

Beyond the hikers, note a sea of cheatgrass, an introduced species that "cheats" native species of water and soil nutrients.

ENDANGERED DIRT
Some advocates of zero-impact recreation suggest "leave only footprints," but in the high desert, this is bad advice. One footprint can destroy decades of growth.

Cryptobiotic crust is the foundation of life in the high desert. It provides a seedbed for the desert plant community and serves as a sponge, retaining the precious moisture of a dry climate. The crust is also the primary source for fixation of nitrogen, which is crucial to all life in the desert. This crust is a complex community of microorganisms, the most important of which are called cyanobacteria.

When mature, cryptobiotic soil has a lumpy, black-tinged crust. In earlier stages the crust is almost invisible. If you step on it, ride on it, or drive on it, it blows away and erodes, and then it takes many years if not decades to recover.

This is a prime reason to stay on trails and roads. If you have to hike off-trail, try to stay on slickrock or in canyon washes to prevent stepping on cryptobiotic crust. Usually when somebody says "watch your step," they have safety in mind, but in Canyonlands, this can mean the preservation of the high desert environment.

Zero impact—and put your ear to the ground in the wilderness and listen carefully. Thousands of people coming behind you are thanking you for your courtesy and good sense.

FalconGuide's Zero-Impact Principles

- Leave with everything you brought in.
- Leave no sign of your visit.
- Leave the landscape as you found it.

Make It a Safe Trip

The Scouts have been guided for decades by what is perhaps the best single piece of safety advice—be prepared! For starters, this means carrying survival and first-aid materials, proper clothing, a compass, and a topographic map—and knowing how to use them.

Perhaps the second-best piece of safety advice is to tell somebody where you're going and when you plan to return. Pilots must file flight plans before every trip, and anybody venturing into a blank spot on the map should do the same. File your "flight plan" with a friend or relative before taking off.

Close behind your flight plan and being prepared with proper equipment is physical conditioning. Being fit not only makes wilderness travel more fun, it makes it safer. To whet your appetite for more knowledge of wilderness safety and preparedness, here are a few more tips:

- Check the weather forecast. Be careful not to get caught at high altitude by a bad storm or in a narrow canyon by a flash flood. Watch cloud formations closely, so you don't get stranded on a ridgeline during a lightning storm. Avoid traveling during prolonged periods of cold weather.
- Avoid traveling alone in the wilderness.
- Keep your party together.
- Know the preventive measures, symptoms, and treatment of hypothermia, the silent killer.
- Study basic survival and first aid before leaving home.
- Don't eat wild plants.
- Before you leave for the trailhead, find out as much as you can about the route, especially the potential hazards.
- Don't exhaust yourself or other members of your party by traveling too far or too fast. Let the slowest person set the pace.
- Don't wait until you're confused to look at your maps. Follow them as you go along, from the moment you start moving up the trail, so you have a continual fix on your location.

The National Park Service has installed ladders throughout the parks to help hikers get over dangerous spots.

- If you get lost, don't panic. Sit down and relax for a few minutes while you carefully check your topo map and take a reading with your compass. Confidently plan your next move. It's often smart to retrace your steps until you find familiar ground, even if you think it might lengthen your trip. Lots of people get temporarily lost in the wilderness and survive—usually by calmly and rationally dealing with the situation.
- Stay clear of all wild animals. Never feed wild animals.
- Take a first-aid kit that includes, at a minimum, the following items: sewing needle, snake-bite kit, aspirin, antibacterial ointment, two antiseptic swabs, two butterfly bandages, adhesive tape, four adhesive strips, four gauze pads, two triangular bandages, codeine tablets, two inflatable splints, moleskin, one roll 3-inch gauze, CPR shield, rubber gloves, and lightweight first-aid instructions.
- Take a survival kit that includes, at a minimum, the following items: compass, whistle, matches in a waterproof container, cigarette lighter, candle, signal mir-

ror, fire starter, aluminum foil, water purification tablets, space blanket, and a flare.

- Last but not least, don't forget that the best defense against unexpected hazards is knowledge.

You Might Never Know What Hit You

The high desert environs of Canyonlands are prone to sudden thunderstorms, especially in spring and summer months. If you get caught by a lightning storm, take special precautions. Remember:

- Lightning can travel far ahead of the storm, so be sure to take cover before the storm hits.
- Don't try to make it back to your vehicle. Instead seek shelter, even if it's only a short way back to the trailhead. It isn't worth the risk. Lightning storms usually don't last long, and from a safe vantage point, you might enjoy the sights and sounds.
- Be especially careful not to get caught on a mountaintop or exposed ridge; under large, solitary trees; in the open; or near standing water.
- Seek shelter in a low-lying area, ideally in a dense stand of small, uniformly sized trees.
- Stay away from anything that might attract lightning, such as metal tent poles, graphite fishing rods, or pack frames.
- Get in a crouch position and place both feet firmly on the ground.
- If you have a pack (without a metal frame) or a sleeping pad with you, put your feet on it for extra insulation against shock.
- Don't huddle together. Instead, sit 50 feet apart, so if somebody gets hit by lightning, others in your party can give first aid.
- If you're in a tent, stay there, in your sleeping bag with your feet on your sleeping pad.

The Silent Killer

Be aware of the danger of hypothermia—a condition in which the body's internal temperature drops below normal. It can lead to mental and physical collapse and death.

Hypothermia is caused by exposure to cold, and is aggravated by wetness, wind, and exhaustion. The moment you begin to lose heat faster than your body produces it, you're suffering from exposure. Your body starts involuntary exercise such as shivering to stay warm and makes involuntary adjustments to preserve normal temperature in vital organs, restricting blood flow in the extremities. Both responses drain your energy reserves. The only way to stop the drain is to reduce the degree of exposure.

With full-blown hypothermia, as energy reserves are exhausted, cold reaches the brain, depriving you of good judgment and reasoning power. You won't be aware

Many trails in both parks follow cairns over expanses of solid slickrock.

that this is happening. You lose control of your hands. Your internal temperature slides downward. Without treatment, this slide leads to stupor, collapse, and death.

To defend against hypothermia, stay dry. When clothes get wet, they lose about 90 percent of their insulating value. Wool loses relatively less heat; cotton, down, and some synthetics lose more. Choose rain clothes that cover the head, neck, body, and legs, and provide good protection against wind-driven rain. Most hypothermia cases develop in air temperatures between 30 and 50 degrees Fahrenheit, but hypothermia can develop in warmer temperatures.

If your party is exposed to wind, cold, and wet, think hypothermia. Watch yourself and others for these symptoms: uncontrollable fits of shivering; vague, slow, slurred speech; memory lapses; incoherence; immobile, fumbling hands; frequent stumbling or a lurching gait; drowsiness (to sleep is to die); apparent exhaustion; and inability to get up after a rest. When a member of your party has hypothermia, he or she may deny any problem. Believe the symptoms, not the victim.

Even mild symptoms demand treatment, as follows:

- Get the victim out of the wind and rain.
- Strip off all wet clothes.

- If the victim is only mildly impaired, give him or her warm drinks. Then get the victim in warm clothes and a warm sleeping bag. Place well-wrapped water bottles filled with heated water close to the victim.
- If the victim is badly impaired, attempt to keep him or her awake. Put the victim in a sleeping bag with another person—both naked. If you have a double bag, put two warm people in with the victim.
- Temperatures are given in Fahrenheit degrees. To convert to Celsius, subtract 32 from the Fahrenheit number, then multiply by ⅝ or .55.

Moab Monthly Climatological Data

Month	Avg. high temp	Avg. low temp	Max. high temp	Max. low temp	# days over 90°F	# days under 32°F	Avg. precip. (inches)	% of annual precip.
Jan.	43.9°	18.8°	67°	1°	0	30	0.5"	5%
Feb.	52.7°	25.1°	75°	1°	0	23	0.5"	5%
March	63.9°	33.3°	86°	19°	0	15	0.9"	9%
April	76.6°	38.9°	92°	26°	2	3	1.2"	12%
May	84.3°	49.4°	97°	34°	10	0	1.1"	11%
June	97.6°	57.9°	108°	38°	28	0	0.1"	1%
July	99.5°	61.9°	109°	50°	29	0	1.2"	12%
Aug	98.6°	61.5°	107°	49°	30	0	0.8"	7%
Sept.	86.1°	50.4°	102°	30°	12	1	0.8"	7%
Oct.	77.1°	40.3°	92°	26°	4	2	1.6"	15%
Nov.	58.4°	31.7°	78°	16°	0	17	1.2"	12%
Dec.	47.9°	21.4°	60°	10°	0	29	0.5"	4%

- Precipitation is given in inches. To convert to centimeters, multiply inches by 2.54.
- Data from Atlas Minerals Weather Station, Moab, Utah, from 1980 through 1990.
- This chart is for an elevation of 4,000 feet. Most of Canyonlands is at a higher elevation and hence will be cooler in both summer and winter.
- Supplied courtesy of William Baron, Curator, Historical Climate Records Office, Northern Arizona University, Flagstaff, Arizona (1991).

Legend

▲	Campground
▲	Campsite
↦	Gate (Locked)
▲	Mountain/Peak
◼	Overlook/Viewpoint
🅿	Parking
⊞	Picnic
■	Point of Interest
▮	Ranger Station
🚻	Restroom
⟲	Spring
🚶	Trailhead
+	UTM grid tic
🛈	Visitor Information
(70)	Interstate
191	U.S. Highway
(313)	State Highway
═══	Interstate
▬▬▬	U.S. Highway
───	Other Paved Road
═══	Gravel Road
= = =	Unimproved Road
▬ ▬ ▬	Trail
▬▬▬	Highlighted Route
■■■■	Shared Trail
─ ·· ─	Intermittent River/Lake
───	River/Creek
▬▬	Lake/Large River
─ ─ ─	Park Boundary

Arches National Park

Compared to many national parks, Arches is small (73,379 acres), but it's also very scenic and very popular. It was designated a national monument in 1929 and then expanded and designated a national park in 1971. The park is open twenty-four hours a day seven days a week. The visitor center is open every day except Christmas from 8:00 A.M. to 4:30 P.M. from September to mid-April and later during summer months. The park has a fifty-two-site campground at Devils Garden, but sites go on a first-come, first-served basis and getting a site can be difficult.

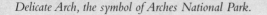

Delicate Arch, the symbol of Arches National Park.

Water, extreme temperatures, and other geologic forces have created the greatest diversity of arches in the world at Arches National Park, along with many other multihued, finely sculpted rock formations. Delicate Arch, perhaps the park's most famous feature, shows up in an endless array of videos, postcards, posters, books, and magazines. However, the numerous arches along the Devils Garden hike, the cathedralistic columns of the Park Avenue, the cavernlike canyons of Fiery Furnace, along with many other spectacular features rival the Delicate Arch (and just about everything else in nature!) for awesome beauty.

A hole in a rock has to have an opening of at least 3 feet to be officially listed as an arch and be given a name. Arches National Park has more than 2,400 arches, a preponderance of arches that makes Arches National Park unique. In fact, there is no place on Earth even remotely like it.

Arches is not for the serious hiker. Instead, it's nicely suited for the visitor who doesn't mind seeing most scenery from the car window or on short walks. The trails offer spectacular scenery, but with one exception, they are all short day hikes. And, unlike Canyonlands National Park, Arches offers limited opportunities to the four-wheeler, with only three short backcountry road sections.

Arches National Park is located 25 miles south of Interstate 70 or 5 miles north of Moab on U.S. Highway 191. The starting points for hikes and drives are referenced from the entrance station.

1 Desert Nature Trail

Start: Arches Visitor Center.
Distance: 0.2 mile.
Type of hike: Very short day hike, loop.
Difficulty: Easy.

Maps: Trails Illustrated Arches National Park and USGS Arches National Park.
Trail contact: Arches National Park, P.O. Box 907, Moab, UT 84532; (435) 259-8161; www.nps.gov/arch.

Finding the trailhead: (See map on page 36.) The visitor center is on your right a short distance after passing through the entrance station.

The Hike

This is a very short (less than 0.2 mile) interpretive trail starting and ending at the Arches Visitor Center. Numbered signs along the way (which correspond with a booklet available at the trailhead) identify and explain the characteristics of the surrounding desert and ecology. Even if you're physically able to do longer hikes and plan to do so later in the day, you might want to take this trail first. It will give you a good base of knowledge about desert plants that you can then try to find on your other hikes.

2 Park Avenue

Start: Park Avenue Parking Area.
Distance: 1 mile.
Type of hike: Short day hike, shuttle or out-and-back.
Difficulty: Easy.

Maps: Trails Illustrated Arches National Park and USGS Arches National Park.
Trail contact: Arches National Park, P.O. Box 907, Moab, UT 84532; (435) 259-8161; www.nps.gov/arch.

Finding the trailhead: (See map on page 36.) The Park Avenue Parking Area is on your left 2.5 miles from the entrance station. The Courthouse Towers Parking Area is on your right 3.7 miles from the entrance station in the shadow of massive Courthouse Towers.

The Hike

The Park Avenue Trail is most aptly named for New York City's famous street. Early travelers noticed a similarity between these sandstone spires and the famous skyscrapers along New York's Park Avenue, and the name stuck. The main difference of course is that the "skyscrapers" of Arches National Park were sculpted by nature.

1 Desert Nature Trail; 2 Park Avenue

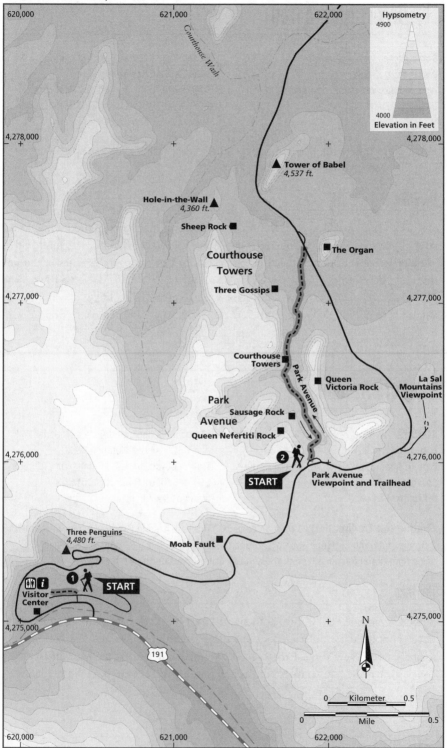

Hypsometry
4900

4000
Elevation in Feet

Courthouse Wash

▲ Tower of Babel
4,537 ft.

Hole-in-the-Wall ▲
4,360 ft.

Sheep Rock ■

■ The Organ

**Courthouse
Towers**

Three Gossips ■

4,278,000

4,277,000

Courthouse
Towers ■

Park Avenue

■ Queen
Victoria Rock

La Sal
Mountains
Viewpoint

**Park
Avenue**

Sausage Rock ■

Queen Nefertiti Rock ■

❷

START

Park Avenue
Viewpoint and Trailhead

4,276,000

Three Penguins
4,480 ft.

▲

Moab Fault ■

❶

START

Visitor
Center

4,275,000

191

N

0   Kilometer   0.5

0   Mile   0.5

Although you can start at either end of this shuttle trail, starting at the south end results in a totally downhill hike. However, if you want to take this shuttle route as you leave the park, start at the north end, and have somebody pick you up at the south end. If you can't arrange a shuttle, this hike is definitely still worth taking, even with double the mileage (still only 2 miles) by going out and back.

You'll really be missing something if you leave Arches without taking this short hike. You can see the Courthouse Towers, Tower of Babel, Three Gossips, the Organ, and other grand "skyscrapers" from the road, but if you don't take this hike, you'll miss the truly stimulating experience of walking among them.

The trail starts out as a concrete path leading to a scenic overlook about 100 yards from the trailhead. From here, a well-defined trail goes through juniper and cactus until it melts into a slickrock dry wash and stays there until just before you return to the main road. The trail disappears, but there's no chance of getting lost.

Park Avenue in Arches National Park is more awe-inspiring than the famous street in New York City.

Stay in the dry wash and follow well-placed cairns to the Courthouse Towers Parking Area.

3 Balanced Rock

Start: Balanced Rock Parking Area.
Distance: 0.2 mile.
Type of hike: Very short day hike, loop.
Difficulty: Easy.

Maps: Trails Illustrated Arches National Park and USGS Arches National Park.
Trail contact: Arches National Park, P.O. Box 907, Moab, UT 84532; (435) 259-8161; www.nps.gov/arch.

Finding the trailhead: (See map on page 39.) The Balanced Rock Parking Area is on the east side of the main park road 9 miles from the entrance station.

The Hike

This is a very short hike, but it's perfect for travelers who would like to stretch their legs without working up a sweat. You can see Balanced Rock and read about it on an interpretive display from near the paved road, but it's not the same as getting up close. The trail makes a short loop around Balanced Rock and returns to the parking area.

The forces of nature sculpted Balanced Rock out of Entrada Sandstone. Technically this is called a "caprock" of harder Slick Rock Member (a type of Entrada Sandstone) perched on a pedestal of softer Dewey Bridge Member (also Entrada Sandstone). The pedestal erodes more quickly than the more resistant caprock. The entire Balanced Rock formation is 128 feet high, and the rock itself measures 55 feet.

Balanced Rock used to have a companion called, of course, Chip-Off-the-Old-Block, but it toppled during the winter of 1975–76. You can still see its pedestal on the south side of Balanced Rock.

3 Balanced Rock; 4 Windows Primitive Loop; 5 Double Arch

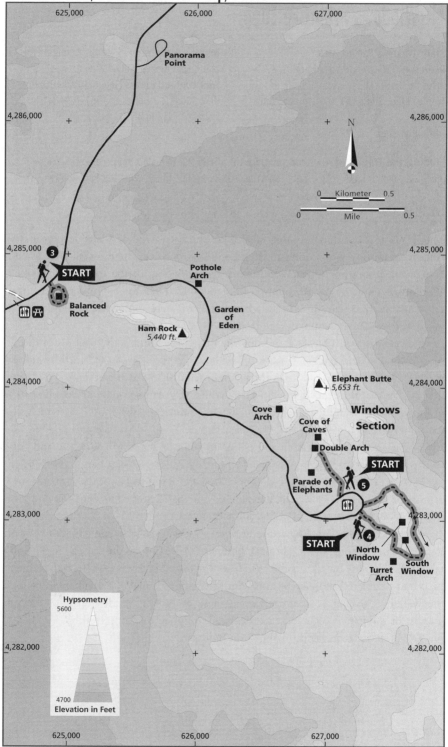

4 Windows Primitive Loop

Start: Windows Parking Area.
Distance: 0.9 mile for out-and-back, 1.25 miles for loop.
Type of hike: Short day hike, out-and-back, or loop.
Difficulty: Easy.

Maps: Trails Illustrated Arches National Park and USGS Arches National Park.
Trail contact: Arches National Park, P.O. Box 907, Moab, UT 84532; (435) 259-8161; www.nps.gov/arch.

Finding the trailhead: (See map on page 39.) Drive 9.2 miles north into the park on the main road until it forks. Take a right (east) and drive 3 miles to the Windows Parking Area.

The Hike

The scenery is sensational on this short hike, but don't expect to have it to yourself. Almost everybody who comes to the park hikes up to see these spectacular arches. When you hear somebody talking about overcrowding in the national parks, the Windows section of Arches often comes to mind. Therefore consider taking this short hike early or late in the day when the crowds are somewhat diminished and you are more likely to find a place to park.

Although it seems like it should be the other way around, the trail heads to the North Window and then to the South Window. On the way to the North Window, you should take a short side trip to the right (south) to see Turret Arch. The Windows are sometimes called the Spectacles, and you can see why. If you hike the primitive loop around the back of the arches, you can see the "nose" on which the spectacles rest.

It's fairly easy to go off-trail and climb up right under North Window and Turret Arch. Do not attempt to climb into South Window. Several people have fallen while trying or have gotten stranded here. Be careful not to fall or damage any vegetation or natural features. Also, hang onto your hat. The strong winds in the area tend to blow it off as soon as you reach either arch.

After you finish marveling at the Windows and Turret Arch, you can retrace your steps back to the parking lot (about 0.9 mile) or you can turn this into a longer walk (about 1.25 miles) by taking the Windows Primitive Loop Trail. The well-defined loop trail starts from the viewpoint of South Window. It makes a small circle around the Windows, giving you another great view of North Window. It also offers a glimpse at the native vegetation of the area. The primitive loop trail hits the parking lot about 50 yards north of the main trailhead.

The Windows.

5 Double Arch

Start: Double Arch Parking Area.
Distance: 0.5 mile.
Type of hike: Short day hike, out-and-back.
Difficulty: Easy.

Maps: Trails Illustrated Arches National Park and USGS Arches National Park.
Trail contact: Arches National Park, P.O. Box 907, Moab, UT 84532; (435) 259-8161; www.nps.gov/arch.

Finding the trailhead: (See map on page 39.) Drive 9.2 miles north into the park on the main road until it forks. Take the right fork for 3 miles to the Windows Parking Area and keep going around a loop in the parking area for about a quarter mile. Park in the Double Arch Parking Area on your right (north).

The Hike

The short (about 0.25 mile one-way), relatively flat hike to Double Arch goes through scattered junipers and oaks. In the spring you might see Utah's state flower, the sego lily, a large, single, cream-colored flower. The trail is well defined and easy to follow all the way. Along the way, off to your left, you can see the series of buttes called the Parade of Elephants.

Double Arch looks sort of average from the parking area, but as you approach, its massiveness starts to sink in. Then, when you get there (and especially if you can climb up right under the arches), the imposing size of the arch becomes absolutely clear. It's the third largest arch opening in the park.

You can lengthen your trip by climbing up under Double Arch, but be careful not to disturb vegetation or natural features. If each person visiting this area left only a tiny mark, it wouldn't take long for the impact to be devastating.

Hikers marveling at majestic Double Arch. ▶

6 Delicate Arch

Start: Wolfe Ranch Parking Area.
Distance: 3 miles.
Type of hike: Day hike, out-and-back.
Difficulty: Moderate.

Maps: Trails Illustrated Arches National Park and USGS Arches National Park.
Trail contact: Arches National Park, P.O. Box 907, Moab, UT 84532; (435) 259-8161; www.nps.gov/arch.

Finding the trailhead: (See map on page 46.) Drive 11.7 miles north into the park on the main road until you see the right-hand turn to Delicate Arch and Wolfe Ranch. Turn right and drive another 1.2 miles to the parking area on your left (north). Look to your right for a lot for oversize vehicles.

The Hike

If you've ever seen a postcard or poster of Arches National Park, you've probably seen Delicate Arch. This amazing arch has become the symbol of Arches National Park, which is somewhat surprising because it's barely visible from the road.

You have three options for viewing this magnificent natural feature. You can take a 1.5-mile trail (3 miles round-trip), which goes right under the arch, or you can go to the Delicate Arch Viewpoint, or take a five-minute walk to a closer viewpoint. If you choose the hiking option, be aware that the trail to Delicate Arch is not a stroll. This is a real hike, and you should be prepared. Bring extra water (a minimum of one quart per person), wear good hiking shoes, and try to avoid the midday heat. There is little shade along this trail. The NPS describes the trail as "moderately strenuous."

At the trailhead you can see the remains of the Wolfe Ranch, settled in 1888 and abandoned in 1910. Shortly after leaving the trailhead, you cross over Salt Wash on a bridge. Right after the bridge, you might notice a large pile of "green stuff" on your right. This is volcanic ash with a high iron content that has gone through a chemical process that gives it this greenish cast. Just after the bridge you can take a short side trip to the left to a Ute petroglyph panel. During the first part of the hike, watch for collared lizards. These large lizards can run on their hind feet when chasing prey.

For the first half mile or so, you hike on a wide, well-defined, mostly level trail. Then the excellent trail disappears, and you start a gradual ascent to Delicate Arch. Most of the rest of the trip is on slickrock, so be alert. You have to follow cairns the rest of the way, and sometimes the "cairns" are only one rock. As you get closer to Delicate Arch, you can see Frame Arch off to your right. This arch forms a perfect "frame" for a photograph of Delicate Arch. If you decide to climb up this short, steep slope to get that photograph, be careful.

Just before you get to Delicate Arch, the trail goes along a ledge for about 200 yards. This section of trail was blasted out of the cliff, and you can still see the bore

Hikers on the ledge just before reaching Delicate Arch.

holes in the rock. If you have children with you, watch them carefully in this section. Just after the ledge ends, you see Delicate Arch with its huge opening (33 feet wide and 45 feet high). You can take an awe-inspiring walk down to right below the arch, but you might ruin somebody's photo. A shot of Delicate Arch with the often snowcapped La Sal Mountains as a backdrop must be one of those photos every professional photographer has to have in his or her file, so one or two shutterbugs are usually setting up tripods for the grand view.

If you prefer the less strenuous option for seeing Delicate Arch, drive past the Wolfe Ranch Parking Area and go another 1.2 miles. From the parking area take one of two short walks—a short (0.5 mile) trail to the top of a small ridge where you can look north for a good view of Delicate Arch, or an even shorter trail to a different viewpoint. These views don't quite compare with being right there, but they're still awe-inspiring.

The first part of the longer viewpoint trail is well defined, but the last part goes over slickrock marked by cairns. There is no sign marking the end of the trail, but you'll know when to stop. At the end of the trail, you're at the edge of a steep cliff that drops down into Winter Camp Wash. You can't hike to the arch from this point.

Delicate Arch

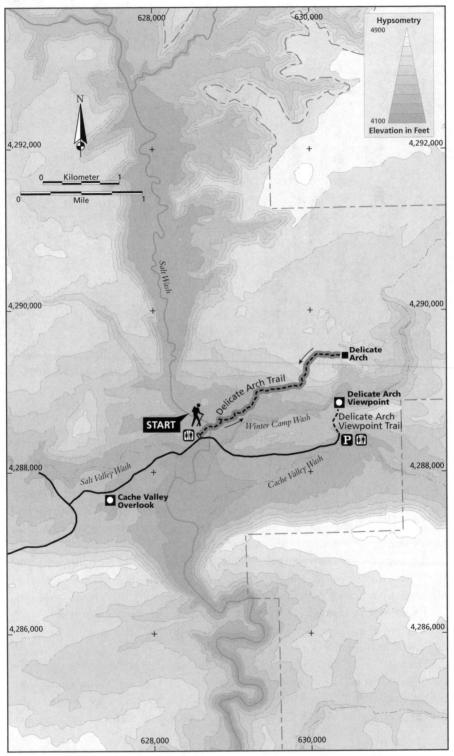

7 Sand Dune Arch

Start: Broken Arch/Sand Dune Arch Parking Area.

Distance: 0.5 mile.

Type of hike: Short day hike, out-and-back.

Difficulty: Easy.

Maps: Trails Illustrated Arches National Park and USGS Arches National Park.

Trail contact: Arches National Park, P.O. Box 907, Moab, UT 84532; (435) 259-8161; www.nps.gov/arch.

Finding the trailhead: (See map on page 49.) Drive north into the park on the main road for 17.5 miles and park along the main road in the Broken Arch/Sand Dune Arch Parking Area.

The Hike

Sand Dune Arch is an easy, short walk nicely suited for groups with children. Even on a hot day, kids will love this place.

Shortly after leaving the trailhead, you hit a junction with the left-hand trail going to Broken Arch. Go right to Sand Dune Arch. Until the junction the trail is well defined. After the junction you enter a narrow canyon (actually the gap between two sandstone fins) and stay there until you see Sand Dune Arch off to your right.

The reason for this arch's name becomes obvious along the way. You walk through deep sand, which can make footing difficult and progress slow. The trail ends right at the arch. Below the arch the sand has collected in a huge "sandbox" that kids love. The area usually stays shaded and coolish, even on a hot summer day. It might be tempting to climb to the top of the arch, but please resist the temptation. Rangers frequently have to rescue people who injured themselves when falling or jumping from the arch.

8 Broken Arch

Start: Devils Garden Campground across from campsite No. 40.
Distance: 1 mile.
Type of hike: Short day hike, loop.
Difficulty: Easy.

Maps: Trails Illustrated Arches National Park and USGS Arches National Park.
Trail contact: Arches National Park, P.O. Box 907, Moab, UT 84532; (435) 259-8161; www.nps.gov/arch.

Finding the trailhead: (See map on page 49.) Drive north into the park on the main road for 19 miles and turn into the Devils Garden Campground. Go to the end of the campground and park along the small loop near the trailhead.

The Hike

The trail, which starts at campsite No. 40 at the end of Devils Garden Campground, goes through sand dunes and slickrock to Broken Arch. In places the trail isn't well defined, but well-placed cairns make it easy to follow all the way. The trail goes right through Broken Arch—a nice place to take a break and study a great piece of nature's art.

You can retrace your steps back to the trailhead from here, but most hikers elect to take the loop trail that continues through the arch and comes back to the campground at campsite No. 51. Along the way you'll see a trail coming in from Sand Dune Arch. If you're interested in adding a mile to your hike, you can take this trail out-and-back to Sand Dune Arch before completing the loop. At the end of the loop, you have to walk about 0.25 mile on the paved campground road back to your vehicle.

7 Sand Dune Arch; 8 Broken Arch; 9 Skyline Arch; 10 Devils Garden

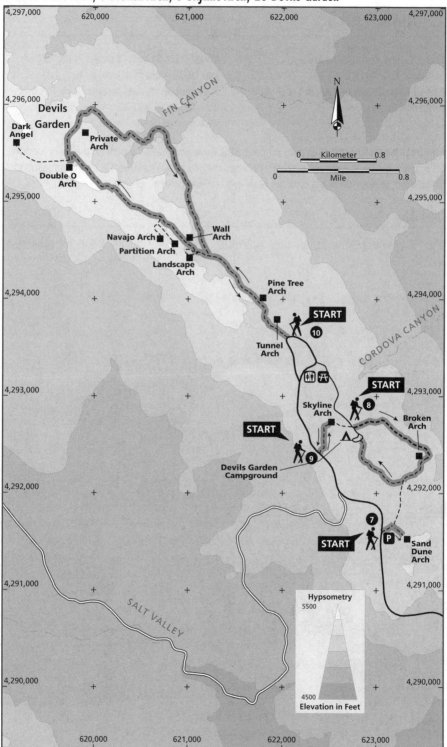

9 Skyline Arch

Start: Skyline Arch Parking Area.
Distance: 0.4 mile.
Type of hike: Short day hike, out-and-back.
Difficulty: Easy.

Maps: Trails Illustrated Arches National Park and USGS Arches National Park.
Trail contact: Arches National Park, P.O. Box 907, Moab, UT 84532; (435) 259-8161; www.nps.gov/arch.

Finding the trailhead: (See map on page 49.) Drive north into the park on the main road for 18.5 miles and park in the Skyline Arch Parking Area. If you see the Devils Garden Campground or Trailhead, you've driven just past the Skyline Arch Parking Area.

The Hike

This is a very easy walk. It's only 0.2 mile to Skyline Arch on a flat, well-defined trail.

Skyline Arch.

True to its name Skyline Arch dominates the horizon for most of the trip. When you get there you can see where a mammoth boulder fell out of the arch on a cold November night in 1940, greatly enlarging the size of the opening. This essentially doubled the size of the arch.

At the base of the arch, it looks as though a trail goes off to your left (north), but this isn't an official trail and doesn't go anywhere. This is a good example of why the NPS encourages hikers to stay on official trails. In the area around Skyline Arch, hikers who should have stayed on the official trail have created several well-defined "social trails."

10 Devils Garden

Start: Devils Garden Trailhead Parking Area.
Distance: 2 miles to Landscape Arch, 4 miles to Double O Arch, or 7.2 miles to Double O Arch returning by the Primitive Loop Trail, including all spur trails to points of interest.
Type of hike: Short out-and-back (to Landscape Arch) or moderately long day hike (primitive loop).

Difficulty: Easy (to Landscape Arch), moderate (to Double O Arch and on the Primitive Loop Trail).
Maps: Trails Illustrated Arches National Park and USGS Arches National Park.
Trail contact: Arches National Park, P.O. Box 907, Moab, UT 84532; (435) 259-8161; www.nps.gov/arch.

Finding the trailhead: (See map on page 49.) Drive north into the park on the main road for 19 miles and park in the large parking area at the Devils Garden Trailhead. The trailhead is at the end of the road where it makes a small loop. Be sure to stay on the loop instead of turning into the Devils Garden Campground.

The Hike

If you take the Primitive Loop Trail and all the short spur trails to nearby arches and other features, this becomes the longest hike on maintained trails in Arches National Park. It's also one of the most spectacular hikes you can take in any national park.

You can hike the entire loop in about 3 hours, but you could—and probably should—spend an entire day checking out the area and relaxing along the way. In any case be sure to carry extra water. Also, you might want to get up early to take this hike to beat the heat—and to be sure you find a parking spot in the large but heavily used parking area.

About a quarter mile from the trailhead, the trail splits. To go to Landscape Arch and Double O Arch and complete the loop, take the left-hand fork. The right-hand fork takes you on a short spur trail down to Pine Tree and Tunnel Arches. If you take this spur trail, it splits again at the bottom of a small hill. Go left to Pine Tree Arch and right to Tunnel Arch. After checking out these two large arches, head back to the main trail.

The truly amazing Landscape Arch on Devils Garden Trail.

About a mile down the main trail, just before you see Landscape Arch and as you descend a series of steps, you see where the Primitive Loop Trail comes in. You can take the loop either way, of course, but this description covers the clockwise route, so take a left at this junction and continue to Landscape Arch.

The hike to Landscape Arch (about 2 miles out-and-back) is akin to the trip to Delicate Arch. It's one of those must-see features of Arches National Park. This first part of the Devils Garden hike is a "super-trail"—flat, easy, doublewide, and usually heavily populated with hikers. Landscape Arch has an opening spanning an incredible 306 feet, which may be the longest stone span in the world. On the geologic time scale, Landscape Arch is a senior citizen among arches in the park. The arch is also famous for the extreme slenderness of its stone span. Don't wait too long to see Landscape Arch. Geologically speaking it's likely to collapse any day. Many people interested in a short hike turn back at Landscape Arch. If you have the time and energy, however, the trail ahead has much more to offer.

After Landscape Arch the trail gets less defined and stays that way. In fact, right after Landscape Arch the trail gets primitive for a short stretch, where it climbs over sandstone slabs and is marked with cairns. It's still easy to follow, though, and the trail all the way to Double O Arch gets lots of use. In this section, you pass Wall Arch on your right. As at Landscape Arch you don't have to leave the main trail to see Wall Arch.

Another 0.25 mile up the trail, you'll see a short spur trail going off to the left to Partition and Navajo Arches. Partition Arch is the arch you can see in the background when you're looking at Landscape Arch. Yes, Partition Arch has a partition, and the spur trail goes right up under the arch and ends, a great place to relax and soak in the view. The trail to Navajo Arch also stops right under the arch, another great place for a break. This arch is shaded and perhaps an even better place than Partition Arch to stop and relax before continuing to Double O Arch.

When you get back on the main trail, it's another 0.5 mile to Double O Arch on a fairly rough trail, mostly on slickrock, and a little hard to follow. Double O Arch is most unusual, one arch on top of another. Just after Double O Arch, you hit a junction with a spur trail heading to the left to Dark Angel. Taking this spur trail

Hiking the Primitive Loop Trail section of Devils Garden Trail.

Hikers headed to Pine Tree Arch on Devils Garden Trail.

adds nearly 1 mile to your trip, but it's worth it to get a close look at this blackish sandstone spike jutting out of the desert landscape.

Also right after Double O Arch, the Primitive Loop Trail heads off to the right. The NPS has marked it CAUTION, PRIMITIVE TRAIL, DIFFICULT HIKING, and the loop section of this hike is about as difficult as the section between Landscape and Partition Arches, which you have already hiked. In winter some sections can be wet or icy, making footing quite slick. If you turn back at this point, you will have seen most of the famous features of the Devils Garden Trail.

About half a mile up the Primitive Loop Trail, watch for a short spur trail going off to the right to Private Arch, the last arch you see on this loop. From here, instead of going from arch to arch as the first part of this trip, the loop trail traverses a beautiful desert environment where you can study the flora and fauna—and probably have it all to yourself. Even though thousands of hikers take the first part of this loop trip, most people choose to retrace their steps on a better trail than brave the primitive loop route.

Miles and Directions

0.25 Spur trail to Tunnel and Pine Tree Arches.

0.8 Landscape Arch, junction with Primitive Loop Trail, turn left.

1.0 Wall Arch.

1.4 Navajo Arch.

1.5 Partition Arch.

2.0 Double O Arch.

2.1 Junction with Primitive Loop Trail, turn right.

2.5 Dark Angel.

2.9 Private Arch.

6.2 Junction with main trail, turn left.

7.2 Devils Garden Trailhead.

11 Tower Arch

Start: Tower Arch Trailhead.
Distance: 2.4 miles.
Type of hike: Short day hike, out-and-back.
Difficulty: Moderate.

Maps: Trails Illustrated Arches National Park and USGS Arches National Park.
Trail contact: Arches National Park, P.O. Box 907, Moab, UT 84532; (435) 259-8161; www.nps.gov/arch.

Finding the trailhead: (See map on page 56.) Turn left (west) onto Salt Valley Road, which leaves the main road 16 miles beyond the entrance station. Follow the road for 7.1 miles until you see a junction with a sign pointing to a left turn to Klondike Bluffs. Take this road for 1.5 miles until it ends at the Tower Arch Trailhead. Be careful not to take the left turn (which leads to a difficult four-wheel-drive road) just before the road to Klondike Bluffs Road.

The Hike

Tower Arch is a short but rugged hike, or as indicated by the sign at the trailhead, a PRIMITIVE TRAIL.

The trail immediately starts to climb to the top of the bluff, up a steep but short incline. After this brief climb the trail continues up and down until you see massive Tower Arch surrounded by a maze of spectacular sandstone spires. Along the way you get great views of the austere Klondike Bluffs on your right.

Part of the trail is on slickrock, so always be watching for the next cairn. The roughest part of the trail, however, goes through two stretches of loose sand near the end of the hike that make hiking uphill difficult. It's easy coming back, though.

Tower Arch

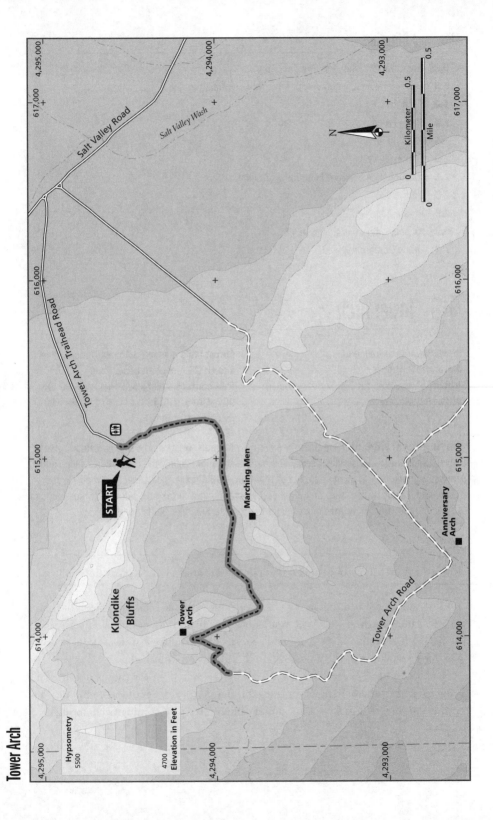

Hiking to Tower Arch with Klondike Bluffs in the background.

You can climb up under the arch and get a great view while taking a deserved rest stop. In spring you'll see the magnificent, snowcapped La Sal Mountains to the east through the arch opening.

The return trip is noticeably easier than the way in. When you're at Tower Arch, you might see a vehicle just to the east. That's because you can drive around on a rough four-wheel-drive road, but those that do miss out on a great hike.

12 Fiery Furnace

Start: Fiery Furnace Parking Area.
Distance: 2 miles.
Type of hike: Ranger-led day hike, loop.
Difficulty: Moderate (ranger-led trips) or difficult (self exploration).

Maps: Trails Illustrated Arches National Park and USGS Arches National Park.
Trail contact: Arches National Park, P.O. Box 907, Moab, UT 84532; (435) 259-8161; www.nps.gov/arch.

Finding the trailhead: Drive north into the park on the main road for 14.5 miles and turn right (east) at well-signed Fiery Furnace Road (just after the Salt Valley Overloo). Park in the Fiery Furnace Parking Area, which is a short drive from the main road.

The Hike

To see the Fiery Furnace area of Arches National Park, you can take a ranger-led tour or take an off-trail adventure on your own. In either case, stop at the visitor center when entering the park to get a permit or to make a reservation for the guided tour and be sure to take water.

Incidentally this area was not named for its average temperature. Actually it belies its name and remains fairly cool even in midsummer due to the many shady canyons. Instead the area was named for the reddish glow it often takes on at sunset, which resembles a furnace.

After a brief orientation talk, a ranger leads the guided tour down one of the trails leaving the parking area. Three hours later you return to the parking area on the other trail. As you walk along the 2-mile loop, the ranger explains the incredible natural history of the area and points out rare plants and semiconcealed arches.

The Fiery Furnace has suffered from its popularity. As a result the NPS imposed special restrictions in 1994 in an attempt to curb a disturbing amount of damage to the fragile resources of the area. If you elect to go exploring on your own, you must talk to a ranger who will help you understand the problems of overuse and discuss getting a permit. The area is a labyrinth of narrow sandstone canyons, and there are no marked trails, making it very difficult to stay oriented.

Two defined trails leave the trailhead, but they soon melt away into a fascinating puzzle of crevasses, fins, and boulders. This maze of canyons may be one of the most difficult areas to hike in the park, but it's also one of the most remarkable. The scenery, especially the steep-sided canyons and weird-shaped rocks, along with several arches and bridges, is unforgettable. You can also find a totally quiet place in the Fiery Furnace to help you forget the stress in your life.

The Fiery Furnace also provides critical habitat for many rare plant species, such as the Canyonlands biscuitroot, so please be intensely careful not to step on black-crusted cryptobiotic soil (desert topsoil) or delicate plant communities. Try

Interpretive rangers lead daily tours into Fiery Furnace.

to walk exclusively on rock or in sandy washes.

For more information contact Arches National Park, P.O. Box 907, Moab, UT 84532; (435) 259–8161; www.nps.gov/arch.

The NPS charges a fee for both ranger-led tours and permits in the Fiery Furnace area.

Because of sensitive and threatened vegetation and the fact that it's easy to get lost in this area, the NPS prefers that no map of the route be included with this hike description.

CANYONLANDS NATIONAL PARK:
Island in the Sky

sland in the Sky is a high mesa wedged between the Colorado and Green Rivers like a natural observation platform. Vistas rival those found anywhere. This district of Canyonlands National Park is the darling of the mountain biker, and mountain-biking tours on the White Rim Road have become intensely popular. During peak seasons campsites along the road are always full, having been reserved many months in advance. However, those without a mountain bike need not worry. Island in the Sky has lots to offer hikers, four-wheelers, or casual tourists driving a rental car.

Although the trail system is not as extensive as in the Needles District, hikers can choose from a variety of well-maintained trails. Trails dropping off the mesa and

The Alcove Spring Trail goes through Trail Canyon with Moses and Zeus in the background.

going to the White Rim Road are for the serious hiker, but the area also has easy and moderate hiking opportunities. Many four-wheelers enjoy the White Rim Road and side roads, but these roads might not present a serious challenge for experts. Tourists with only a day or two to spend here can view some fantastic scenery from the main paved roads in the park. They can supplement their brief visit with several excellent short hikes on the mesa (Grand View, White Rim Overlook, Mesa Arch, Aztec Butte, Whale Rock, or Upheaval Dome Overlook).

Rangers at the Island in the Sky Visitor Center (on your right about a mile past the entrance station) can answer your questions about the natural features and recreational opportunities found in the Island in the Sky District of Canyonlands National Park.

To reach Island in the Sky from Moab, drive north on U.S. Highway 191 10 miles to Highway 313. To reach the same point from farther north, drive 22 miles south from Interstate 70. Once on Highway 313, drive southwest 25 miles to the Island in the Sky entrance station.

13 Neck Spring

Start: Neck Spring Trailhead at Shafer Canyon Overlook.
Distance: 5 miles.
Type of hike: Day hike, loop.
Difficulty: Moderate.

Maps: Trails Illustrated Island in the Sky and USGS Musselman Arch.
Trail contact: Canyonlands National Park, 2282 South West Resource Boulevard, Moab, UT 84532; (435) 719-2313; www.nps.gov/cany.

Finding the trailhead: (See map on page 65.) Drive 0.8 mile south of the Island in the Sky Visitor Center and turn left (east) into the Shafer Canyon Overlook Parking Area.

The Hike

The Neck has historical significance. Here the Island in the Sky plateau narrows to about 40 feet with sheer cliffs dropping off on both sides. This natural phenomenon allowed early ranchers who ran livestock in the area (before the park was created) to control the entire 43-square-mile mesa with one 40-foot fence across this narrow spot, later named the Neck. Nature is also making a play at The Neck. Erosion is gradually wearing away the already narrow entrance to Island in the Sky. Sometime in the future Island in the Sky might really be an island.

One pleasant characteristic of the Neck Spring Trail is that it's a loop, one of the few in the Island in the Sky area. Most trails here are out-and-back or shuttles from road to road. This trail description follows the counterclockwise route. For more information you can get a small brochure on the Neck Spring area at the visitor center or trailhead.

For hikers looking for a moderate, half-day hike this trail is ideal. The trail is well defined the entire way, with good footing (only one small slickrock section) and only minor elevation gain. Parts of the trail parallel the main road, but you're far enough away that you hardly notice. You will notice, however, the panoramic views from the trail.

The Neck Spring area allows hikers to experience a wide variety of high desert habitats in a small area. In spring the area often turns into a wildflower garden, so wildflower buffs will love this trail.

After leaving the trailhead, immediately cross the main road and continue on the trail on the other side. The first part of the trail is actually an old road built by ranchers who used Neck Spring as a water source. Along this section of trail, you'll notice signs of past ranching activities, such as pipes and water troughs. The trail then drops down in elevation and angles to the left toward Neck Spring but not directly to the spring. You can easily see it, however. It's tempting to bushwhack over to the spring, but please enjoy it from a distance. This trail gets heavy use, and this is an extremely fragile area.

Neck Spring Trail.

From the trail you'll notice a change in the vegetation, with species such as Gambel oak and maidenhair fern able to exist in this area with its extra moisture and shade. Also watch for hummingbirds, deer, and other wild animals who frequent the area.

After Neck Spring the trail climbs slightly as you head toward the second major spring in the area, Cabin Spring. At this spring you see the same type of vegetative change as you did at Neck Spring—and a few aging signs of past ranching activity. Shortly after Cabin Spring, you face a short but steep climb up to the Island in the Sky mesa. The trail gets a little rough here, some of it on slickrock. When on top, you get a grand vista of Upper Taylor Canyon and the Henry Mountains off in the distance.

The last part of the trail follows the rim of the plateau directly above Cabin Spring and Neck Spring and through Gray's Pasture, a grassy bench used for cattle grazing until 1975. With no livestock grazing, the area's native grasses have begun to recover and now provide food for native species only. After passing by the top of Neck Spring, cross the main road again and follow the old road cut about a half mile back to the parking area. Be careful crossing and walking along the road.

Neck Spring

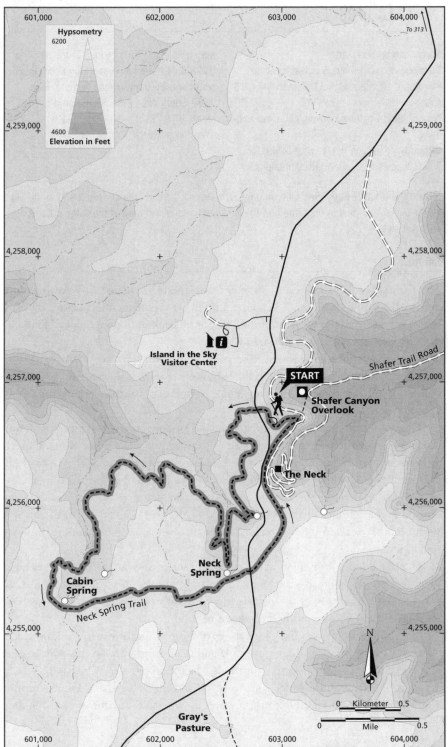

Hypsometry
6200

Elevation in Feet
4600

To 313

601,000 602,000 603,000 604,000

4,259,000

4,258,000

4,257,000

4,256,000

4,255,000

Island in the Sky
Visitor Center

START

Shafer Canyon
Overlook

Shafer Trail Road

The Neck

Neck
Spring

Cabin
Spring

Neck Spring Trail

Gray's
Pasture

N

0   Kilometer   0.5

0   Mile   0.5

14 Lathrop

Start: Lathrop Trailhead.
Distance: To canyon rim, 5 miles; to White Rim Road, 10 miles; to the Colorado River, 18 miles.
Type of hike: Day hike or overnighter, out-and-back.
Difficulty: To canyon rim, easy; to White Rim Road, difficult; to Colorado River, moderate.

Maps: Trails Illustrated Island in the Sky and USGS Musselman Arch and Monument Basin.
Trail contact: Canyonlands National Park, 2282 South West Resource Boulevard, Moab, UT 84532; (435) 719-2313; www.nps.gov/cany.

Finding the trailhead: (See map on page 67.) Drive 2.2 miles south of the Island in the Sky Visitor Center and park in the turnoff on the left (east) side of the road at the Lathrop Canyon Trailhead sign.

The Hike

The Lathrop Trail is significantly different than the other trails that leave Island in the Sky for White Rim Road. It goes 2.5 miles on top of the mesa before the trail heads down toward the White Rim, and the climb back up is more gradual than the Wilhite, Gooseberry, or Murphy Basin Trails.

If you want a nice, flat, easy day hike, go to the canyon rim. After you take a break and enjoy the view, return to the trailhead. Another option is arranging a personal shuttle so you can be picked up on White Rim Road, wisely avoiding the climb back up to the mesa.

The hike starts out through a flat grassland of peppergrass and ricegrass (both native species) with meadowlarks singing in the background and not even a juniper to break up the grassy sea. After a mile you leave the ocean of grass and head off over mostly slickrock with a few stretches of loose sand and drop gradually in elevation until you reach the canyon rim. Here you get a grand view of Lathrop Canyon and a glimpse of the mighty Colorado River far below. You can also see White Rim Road and the well-named Airport Tower, a dominant landmark off to your right.

The trail doesn't drop right off the rim into a series of switchbacks (as other trails from the mesa do). Instead it angles off to the right (south) on a ledge and then starts switchbacking gradually down a side canyon to Lathrop Canyon. You can see the trail far below as you gradually drop down to it.

After about 1 mile on the old jeep road, the trail heads east on a little ridge between two canyons for about a half mile and then drops into the dry wash of one of them, which is where you stay for the last half mile or so to White Rim Road. When you get there find a nice rock to sit on and marvel at the awesome Airport Tower and the beautiful cliffs you just came down—and, of course, start thinking

Lathrop

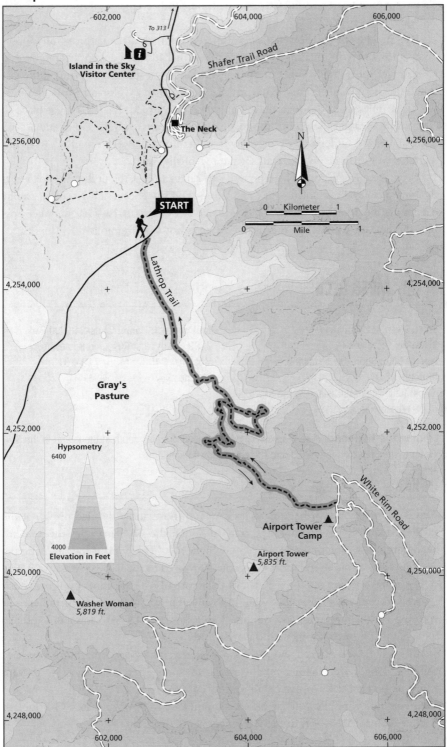

about climbing back up (unless you bribed somebody to pick you up or leave your vehicle here).

Backpacking is not allowed above White Rim Road in the Lathrop and Gooseberry areas, but you can camp below the road in Lathrop Canyon (as long as you ask a ranger about the specifics of this backpacking zone and get a permit at the visitor center in advance). Then you can hike down to the Colorado River the next day. It's 4 miles from the road on a four-wheel-drive road. There's a great place to take a long break at the end of the road, a picnic area with three tables and a vault toilet all nestled under a grove of willows and cottonwoods. The road is easy walking after you drop below the cliffs (at the top of the road).

Even though you might be tempted, you can't camp at the end of the road near the picnic tables. This violates park regulations, and since it's in a big wash, it can be dangerous, too. Don't be too daunted at the cliffs as you walk back. Remember how easy the descent was, which means the ascent is not too strenuous.

15 Mesa Arch

Start: Mesa Arch Trailhead.
Distance: 0.5 mile.
Type of hike: Short day hike, loop.
Difficulty: Easy.
Maps: Trails Illustrated Island in the Sky and USGS Musselman Arch.

Trail contact: Canyonlands National Park, 2282 South West Resource Boulevard, Moab, UT 84532; (435) 719-2313; www.nps.gov/cany.

Finding the trailhead: (See map on page 70.) Drive 6.3 miles south of the Island in the Sky Visitor Center and turn left (east) into the Mesa Arch Parking Area.

The Hike

This is a perfect trail for beginners. It's easy and short, and a detailed display at the trailhead explains how to hike the trail. Although the NPS manages this trail for beginners, it has something for everybody. Signs identify key plant species along the way, and halfway along the short loop, you are treated to spectacular Mesa Arch. The arch is right on the edge of a 500-foot cliff, part of a 1,200-foot drop into Buck Canyon. You can get a keyhole view of White Rim Country through the arch. If you step back a few steps, you can also frame the lofty La Sal Mountains (usually snow-topped in the spring) with the arch.

The trail is well marked and partly on slickrock. It's an easy hike, but if you have children along, watch them carefully around the arch. There is no fence to prevent a sure-to-be-fatal fall. Do not climb on the arch.

If you look carefully you can also see another arch from Mesa Arch Overlook—Washer Woman Arch—off to the left when facing the arch.

Hikers taking a break at Mesa Arch where they get a sweeping view of the White Rim east of Island in the Sky.

16 Aztec Butte

Start: Aztec Butte Trailhead.
Distance: 1.5 miles.
Type of hike: Day hike, out-and-back.
Difficulty: Moderate.
Maps: Trails Illustrated Island in the Sky and USGS Musselman Arch and Upheaval Dome.

Trail contact: Canyonlands National Park, 2282 South West Resource Boulevard, Moab, UT 84532; (435) 719-2313; www.nps.gov/cany.

Finding the trailhead: (See map on page 70.) Drive 6.5 miles south of the Island in the Sky Visitor Center and turn right (west) onto Upheaval Dome Road. Go another 0.8 mile and turn right (north) into the Aztec Butte Parking Area.

The Hike

This hike can be deceptively difficult. The first two-thirds of the trail are well defined and on packed sand, but near the end of the hike, you follow cairns as you

15 Mesa Arch; 16 Aztec Butte; 17 Wilhite

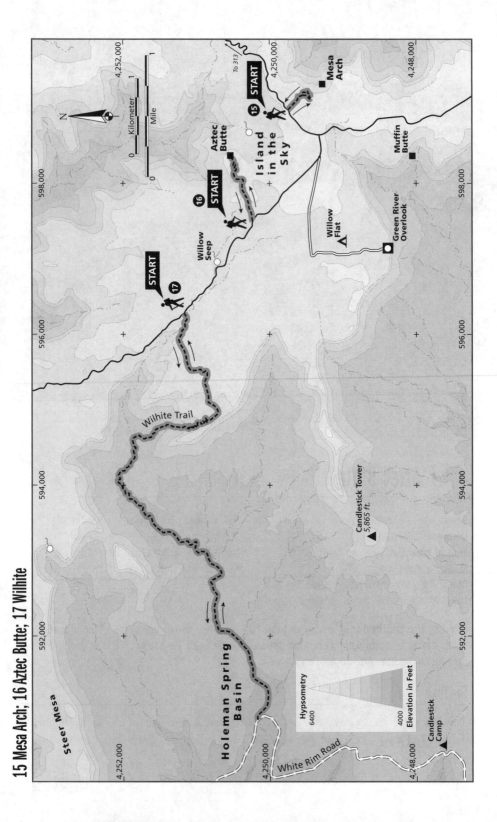

Aztec Butte.

climb about 200 feet up a difficult slickrock slope. The climb up the slickrock slope to the top of the butte is more difficult than ascending Whale Rock, and there are no handrails. Make sure you have appropriate shoes, and be careful.

Once on top you can see an ancestral Puebloan structure called a granary. Don't touch or enter the structure. You can also enjoy some great vistas, particularly the view toward the head wall of massive Trail Canyon to the northwest.

Option: On the way back you can climb up and around the top of a similar butte between Aztec Butte and the trailhead. If you want to take this option, watch for a trail veering off to the west just before you start going around the other, unnamed butte.

17 Wilhite

Start: Wilhite Trailhead.
Distance: 10 miles.
Type of hike: Long day hike or overnighter, out-and-back.
Difficulty: Strenuous.

Maps: Trails Illustrated Island in the Sky and USGS Upheaval Dome.
Trail contact: Canyonlands National Park, 2282 South West Resource Boulevard, Moab, UT 84532; (435) 719-2313; www.nps.gov/cany.

Finding the trailhead: (See map on page 70.) Drive 6.5 miles south of the Island in the Sky Visitor Center and turn right (west) onto Upheaval Dome Road. Go another 2.1 miles to the Wilhite Parking Area at the trailhead sign on the left (south) side of the road.

The Hike

Like other trails leaving Island in the Sky, the Wilhite hike includes a big hill. Although the Gooseberry Trail has the reputation of being the toughest climb in Island in the Sky, the Wilhite has more elevation change (1,600 feet compared to 1,400 feet for Gooseberry). However, that elevation change is spread out over more miles of trail.

The first mile of the hike is easy walking on a nicely defined trail with a few short sections of loose sand and slickrock. Then the trail veers off to the right at the top of the head wall of Holeman Spring Canyon. Like other trails that drop over the "edge of the sky," the view can be somewhat daunting when you realize you have to climb down and then, later, up the steep cliff. However, looks can be deceiving. The NPS has expertly routed the trail down the canyon wall to make it safe and used stairs and switchbacks to minimize the steep grade. All the way down you get great views of expansive Holeman Spring Basin.

At the bottom of the big descent, the trail follows the flat, blackbrush–dotted flats for about a half mile before angling off to the left toward awesome Candlestick Butte. The trail then follows the rim of a canyon for another 0.5 mile before dropping off the rim to the north toward Steer Mesa and then into the dry wash of a small, unnamed canyon. The trail follows the canyon bottoms the rest of the way. In some sections cairns are scarce, but don't fret. The trail stays in the dry wash the entire last 2 miles to White Rim Road. If you're backpacking you can easily find a campsite in this area, but be sure to camp out of the wash for your own safety.

When you hit the road, the dry wash you've been hiking turns into a beautiful slot canyon. If you have some energy left, hike down the slot canyon. It's cool down there, and you can usually find pools of water. If you're staying overnight in the area, this makes a great day hike.

On the way back don't fall asleep on your feet and get in the wrong canyon wash. The canyon the trail follows forks several times. Go left at the first two forks,

Mountain bikers and support vehicles parked at the junction with White Rim Road and Wilhite Trail for a short hike down a slot canyon.

right on the next two, then one more left turn before climbing out of the dry wash. Each fork is clearly marked with cairns, but if you suddenly wake up and realize you haven't seen a cairn for a while, you could have taken a wrong turn. If so, backtrack to the last fork and watch for cairns. Also, be alert not to miss the last turn out of the canyon. The trail takes a sharp right, and it's easy to miss it and continue up the dry wash.

18 Alcove Spring

Start: Alcove Spring Trailhead.
Distance: 10 miles.
Type of hike: Long day hike or overnighter, out-and-back.
Difficulty: Strenuous.

Maps: Trails Illustrated Island in the Sky and USGS Upheaval Dome.
Trail contact: Canyonlands National Park, 2282 South West Resource Boulevard, Moab, UT 84532; (435) 719–2313; www.nps.gov/cany.

Finding the trailhead: (See map on page 76.) Drive 6.5 miles south of the Island in the Sky Visitor Center and turn right (west) onto Upheaval Dome Road. Go another 3.3 miles to the Alcove Spring Parking Area at the trailhead sign on the right (north) side of the road.

The alcove on Alcove Spring Trail.

The Hike

The Alcove Spring Trail starts dropping immediately, but not as steeply as the "big drops" of Wilhite, Murphy, and Gooseberry. The first mile of the trail down from Island in the Sky is a little rocky, but there are lots of steps installed to make hiking down and climbing back up easier. The last 4 miles is easy "wash walking."

The trail gradually switchbacks down with one long stretch along an absolutely massive cliff with an enormous, amphitheater-like alcove for which the trail is named. After about a mile the well-defined trail levels out, angling to the left before heading down into Trail Canyon. In another mile or so, the trail dips into the dry wash of Trail Canyon and stays there until you reach the end of Taylor Canyon Road. Trail Canyon is a big, broad valley with sensational cliffs on both sides.

Once you're in the dry wash, follow it the rest of the way. Some long stretches don't have cairns, but don't fret. The trail stays right in the dry wash. During the last mile you get great views of Zeus and Moses and Aphrodite, awesome spires of rock on the north horizon—the darlings of rock climbers everywhere.

If you're backpacking you won't have any trouble finding a good spot in Trail Canyon. You can also go up into Upper Taylor Canyon to camp.

Just as Trail Canyon merges with Taylor Canyon, the trail leaves the dry wash. This turn is easy to miss, so have your topo map out and watch for cairns at about two o'clock. From here, it's only about a quarter mile on a defined trail to the Moses Trailhead. If you miss this turn, you'll come out at Taylor Camp, and you can walk back from there about a quarter mile to the trailhead.

On the way back, the point where you leave the dry wash is well marked with cairns, so you shouldn't miss it.

18 Alcove Spring; 19 Whale Rock

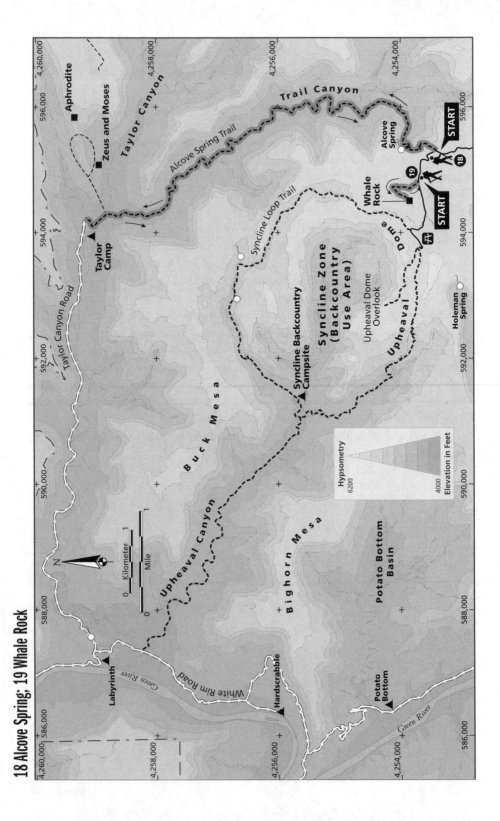

19 Whale Rock

Start: Whale Rock Trailhead.
Distance: 1 mile.
Type of hike: Day hike, out-and-back.
Difficulty: Moderate.
Maps: Trails Illustrated Island in the Sky and USGS Upheaval Dome.

Trail contact: Canyonlands National Park, 2282 South West Resource Boulevard, Moab, UT 84532; (435) 719-2313; www.nps.gov/cany.

Finding the trailhead: (See map on page 76.) Drive 6.5 miles south of the Island in the Sky Visitor Center and turn right (west) onto Upheaval Dome Road. Go another 3.9 miles to the Whale Rock Parking Area at the trailhead sign on the right (north) side of the road.

Handrails help hikers reach the top of Whale Rock.

The Hike

If you want a great view of the entire Island in the Sky area, take the short climb to the top of Whale Rock. From there you get a 360-degree panoramic look at the entire region. Plan on spending some extra time at the top to study all the interesting geologic formations.

The trail goes over slickrock most of the way, but it's carefully marked with cairns and handrails. And yes, if you use a little imagination, this rock outcrop sort of resembles a big old whale.

20 Syncline Loop

Start: Upheaval Dome Parking Area.
Distance: 8 miles.
Type of hike: Long day hike or overnighter, loop.
Difficulty: Strenuous.

Maps: Trails Illustrated Island in the Sky and USGS Upheaval Dome.
Trail contact: Canyonlands National Park, 2282 South West Resource Boulevard, Moab, UT 84532; (435) 719-2313; www.nps.gov/cany.

Finding the trailhead: (See map on page 80.) Drive 6.5 miles south of the Island in the Sky Visitor Center and turn right (west) onto Upheaval Dome Road. Go another 4.8 miles to the Upheaval Dome Picnic Area at the end of the road. The trailhead is at the west end of the picnic area.

The Hike

This trail is the best choice for a long loop in this district. With two exceptions (Neck Spring and Murphy), all other long trails in Island in the Sky are out-and-back hikes. Try for an early start, especially if you plan to cover this trail all in one day. This can be a long, hot day hike in canyon country. Be sure to bring plenty of water: the NPS recommends one gallon per person per day.

The entire Syncline area has a fascinating—and controversial—geological history. Some geologists call Upheaval Dome "the most peculiar structural feature in southeastern Utah." The origin of the dome is the source of endless debate. For some mysterious reason, rocks formerly buried a mile underground are now on the surface in the crater. The two most common theories—the "salt dome" theory and the "meteorite impact" theory—are explained in a brochure available at the trailhead and visitor center. This trail circles the mysterious crater.

About 100 yards up the trail, the Crater View Trail goes straight, and the loop trails go to the left and right. If you're going the clockwise route, as described here, take a left. The first 1.5 miles of the trail are very pleasant—flat, well defined,

The view west from the Syncline Loop Trail.

and easy walking. Then you start a steep descent into Upheaval Canyon. For the next mile, the trail drops abruptly. Some sections are rocky and rough with short switchbacks, but it's still easy to follow. Most of the 1,300-foot elevation loss occurs in this mile. This is a fairly good reason to take the clockwise route. You'll notice that the climb up to the trailhead on the other side of the crater is not quite as steep.

Follow the canyon wash for about another mile to the junction with the Upheaval Canyon Trail. Here the Upheaval Canyon Trail takes a sharp left and heads off to the west toward the Green River. You take a right and head northeast up the Syncline Valley.

Immediately after the junction, you go up a short but steep hill that gets you out of the Upheaval Canyon dry wash and onto a defined trail. Just before the hill, the trail appears to split. You'll be tempted to take the right-hand fork, which is level and avoids the steep incline. Sorry, this isn't the official trail, so take a left and climb the hill. The right fork goes off to the east about 1.5 miles into the depths of the crater (a nice side trip, if you have enough energy and time left).

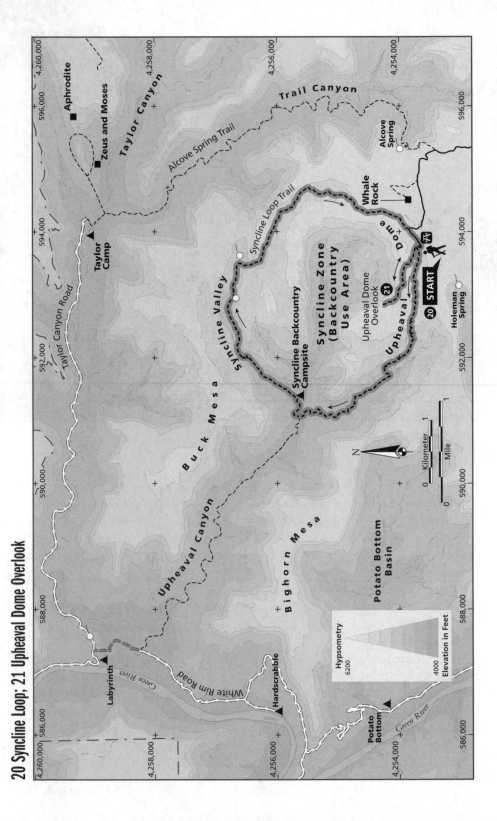

Some sections of the Syncline Loop Trail follow the dry wash.

After you get to the top of the hill, the trail goes by the designated Syncline Backcountry Campsite and then stays nearly level for about a half mile as it follows a grassy bench along the streambed.

In about another half mile, the trail drops into the dry wash of Syncline Valley and starts up a narrow canyon with massive Upheaval Dome on the right and the cliffs leading up to Buck Mesa on the left. This is a beautiful canyon highlighted by a few large cottonwood trees. In the spring you might see intermittent pools of water.

For the next mile or so, you climb steeply and gain most of the elevation you lost a few miles back. Near the top of the canyon is one very steep stretch. After the short steep section, the trail keeps climbing, but it's gradual. You go through an area of lush and diverse vegetation, including a stand of tall trees. At about the 6.5-mile mark, the trail forks. There is a short spur trail that goes off to the right to a spring coming out of an alcove—a great spot for a lunch break.

From here the trail continues to gradually climb all the way to the trailhead, sometimes following the canyon wash. In the last 1.5 miles, you go over some slick-rock sections, some of them moderately steep, so be careful.

Miles and Directions

0.1 Junction with Crater View Trail, turn left.

1.5 Start of steep descent.

3.2 Junction with Upheaval Canyon Trail, turn right.

3.5 Syncline Backcountry Campsite.

8.0 Upheaval Dome Trailhead.

21 Upheaval Dome Overlook

Start: Upheaval Dome Parking Area.
Distance: 1 mile.
Type of hike: Short day hike, out-and-back.
Difficulty: Moderate.
Maps: Trails Illustrated Island in the Sky and USGS Upheaval Dome.

Trail contact: Canyonlands National Park, 2282 South West Resource Boulevard, Moab, UT 84532; (435) 719-2313; www.nps.gov/cany.

Hikers at the Upheaval Dome Overlook interpretive display.

Finding the trailhead: (See map on page 80.) Drive 6.5 miles south of the Island in the Sky Visitor Center and turn right (west) onto Upheaval Dome Road. Go another 4.8 miles to the Upheaval Dome Picnic Area at the end of the road. The trailhead is at the west end of the picnic area.

The Hike

This is a great way to observe and study the geological wonders of the Upheaval Dome area without taking the arduous 8-mile loop. In fact, you get a better view of the mysterious crater from this short trail.

About 100 yards up the trail from the parking lot, the loop trails break off to the left and right. Continue straight. The trail climbs the entire 0.5 mile distance to the first scenic viewpoint located on a slickrock outcrop. The NPS has provided an excellent interpretive display at the end of the trail that explains the geology of the area.

The trail continues on to a second slickrock viewpoint that gives you an even better look at the Upheaval Dome area. This increases the length of the trip to 2.5 miles, but the hike between the first and second overlook is only a gradual upgrade. Both unfenced viewpoints drop off sharply on the west side, so be careful and keep children under close supervision.

22 Upheaval Canyon

Start: Upheaval Canyon Trailhead on the White Rim Road (high-clearance, four-wheel-drive vehicle required).
Distance: 6 miles.
Type of hike: Day hike or overnighter, out-and-back.

Difficulty: Moderate.
Maps: Trails Illustrated Island in the Sky and USGS Upheaval Dome.
Trail contact: Canyonlands National Park, 2282 South West Resource Boulevard, Moab, UT 84532; (435) 719-2313; www.nps.gov/cany.

Finding the trailhead: (See map on page 84.) From the entrance station drive White Rim Road for 69.1 miles and park at the parking area on the left (west) side of the road. You can also reach the trailhead from the north, 3.1 miles from the park boundary.

The Hike

This is the longest hike on a trail accessed only by White Rim Road. It's a great trail, mostly on packed sand. The first part of Upheaval Canyon is a broad open valley, and the trail cuts off the wide meanders. After the first mile or so, it drops into the dry wash. The broad valley you saw at the first part of the hike gradually becomes a narrow, twisting canyon just before you reach the junction with the Syncline Loop Trail.

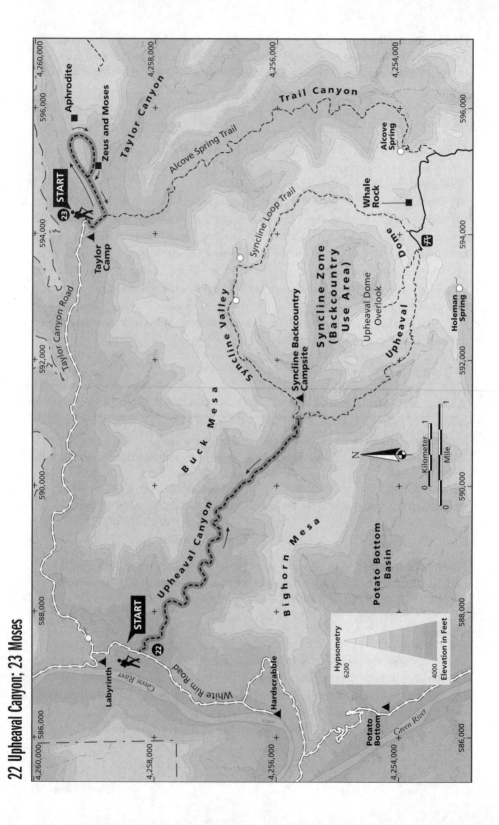

23 Moses

Start: End of Taylor Canyon Road.
Distance: 2 miles.
Type of hike: Day hike, out-and-back.
Difficulty: Moderate.
Maps: Trails Illustrated Island in the Sky and USGS Upheaval Dome.

Trail contact: Canyonlands National Park, 2282 South West Resource Boulevard, Moab, UT 84532; (435) 719-2313; www.nps.gov/cany.

Finding the trailhead: (See map on page 84.) Drive to the end of Taylor Canyon Road, park in the parking area, and walk less than a quarter mile east to the point where both the Moses Trail and the Alcove Spring Trail start and end. You need a four-wheel-drive vehicle to reach this trailhead.

The Hike

This is a new trail not shown on many maps, but you can ask about it at the visitor center. It climbs up and around the Zeus and Moses spires, and then goes through the little pass between Moses and a smaller spire called Aphrodite (unnamed on the maps), which gets you up close and personal to these awe-inspiring formations. Have lunch on the little pass and enjoy views into both forks of Taylor Canyon.

It's a healthy climb to the base of the formations. Use caution hiking the loop around them. If you start thinking this is risky, think of the people who climb all the way to the top. They make this look like a walk in a shopping mall.

24 Alcove Spring/Syncline Loop

Start: Alcove Spring Trailhead.
Distance: 19.6 miles (can be shortened to 18.4 miles).
Type of hike: Multiday backpacking trip, loop.
Difficulty: Strenuous.

Maps: Trails Illustrated Island in the Sky and USGS Upheaval Dome.
Trail contact: Canyonlands National Park, 2282 South West Resource Boulevard, Moab, UT 84532; (435) 719-2313; www.nps.gov/cany.

Finding the trailhead: (See map on page 86.) Drive 6.5 miles south of the Island in the Sky Visitor Center and turn right (west) onto Upheaval Dome Road. Go another 3.3 miles to the Alcove Spring Parking Area at the trailhead sign on the right (north) side of the road. The Upheaval Dome Trailhead is another 1.2 miles down the road.

Alcove Spring/Syncline Loop

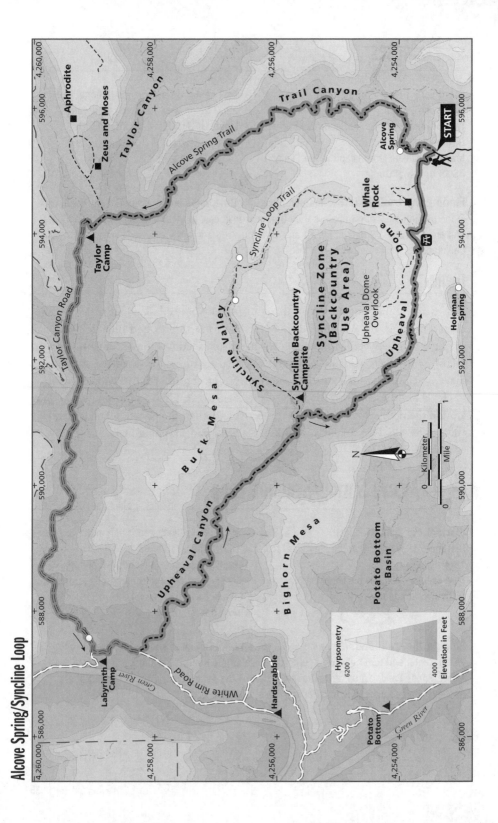

The Hike

Regrettably, the Island in the Sky District doesn't have many long backpacking loops. Instead, most of the long hikes here are out-and-back. However, you can create one very nice loop trip by combining the Alcove Spring, Upheaval Canyon, and part of the Syncline Loop Trails with sections of Taylor Canyon Road and a short section of White Rim Road.

This loop requires a minimum of two nights out, but three nights would leave more time to enjoy the area. The loop can, of course, be taken in either direction, but this description covers the counterclockwise route. There are two ways to shorten the trip. If you're fortunate enough to have two vehicles in your party, leave one at the Upheaval Dome Trailhead so you don't have to hike the last 1.2 miles on paved road back to your vehicle at the Alcove Spring Trailhead. Also, you can take the right (south) turn when you get to the Syncline Loop, which also cuts 1.2 miles off your trip. This route description takes the left (north) route.

Fortunately you have some great choices for both campsites and side trips. You can camp in several side canyons, but not at the designated vehicle campsites (Taylor Canyon or Labyrinth), which are reserved for vehicle campers. You can also camp at the Syncline Backcountry Campsite. Other options for overnight stays include camping in Trail Canyon, Upper Taylor Canyon, The Big Draw, Upheaval Bottom, and Upheaval Canyon. A must-see side trip is to Moses, a 1-mile loop around the famous spire. Perhaps the best second choice is the 3-mile walk (round-trip) into the Upheaval Dome Crater, which leaves from the junction of Syncline Loop Trail and Upheaval Canyon Trail. You can also take side trips up The Big Draw, into Upper Taylor Canyon, and along the Green River. See the chart following this entry for a few suggestions for your itinerary.

When you get to the junction of Upheaval Canyon Trail and Syncline Loop Trail, plan on some extra time to figure out all the signs and trails in the area. There are at least two well-defined but unofficial trails that can get you off track. The officially designated Syncline Backcountry Campsite is off to the left (north) about a quarter mile from the first junction and right along the official trail taking the counterclockwise route around Upheaval Dome.

Miles and Directions

4.7 Trail Canyon and Taylor Canyon merge.

5.0 End of Taylor Canyon Road and Moses Trailhead.

5.2 Taylor Vehicle Campsite.

5.8 The Big Draw.

9.9 White Rim Road.

10.0 Labyrinth Vehicle Campsite.

10.6 Upheaval Canyon Trailhead.

13.6 Syncline Loop/Upheaval Dome Loop Trail.

13.9 Syncline Backcountry Campsite.

18.4 Upheaval Dome Trailhead.

19.6 Alcove Spring Trailhead (on paved road).

Length of Trip	Overnight Stay	Miles Per Day	Side Trips
Two nights	1—The Big Draw 2—Upheaval Canyon or Syncline Backcountry Campsite	1—6-7 miles 2—6-7 miles 3—6-7 miles	Moses Upheaval Crater
Three nights	1—The Big Draw 2—Upheaval Canyon 3—Syncline Campsite	1—6-7 miles 2—4-5 miles 3—3-4 miles 4—5-6 miles	Moses Along Green River Upheaval Crater

25 Murphy Basin

Start: Murphy Trailhead.
Distance: 10 miles.
Type of hike: Long day hike or overnighter, loop.
Difficulty: Strenuous.

Maps: Trails Illustrated Island in the Sky and USGS Monument Basin and Turks Head.
Trail contact: Canyonlands National Park, 2282 South West Resource Boulevard, Moab, UT 84532; (435) 719-2313; www.nps.gov/cany.

Finding the trailhead: (See map on page 89.) Drive 8.6 miles south from the Island in the Sky Visitor Center and park at the pullout at the Murphy Trailhead.

The Hike

Unlike most trails in the Island in the Sky District, Murphy Basin is a nice loop instead of an out-and-back route. A pleasant mile-long walk on White Rim Road connects the Murphy Hogback to the Murphy Wash Trails to complete the loop. This trail description follows the counterclockwise route, which allows you to walk down instead of up a hill on White Rim Road.

From the trailhead you follow a recently abandoned road for about a half mile to the former trailhead and parking area and junction with the Murphy Point Trail. From here the trail stays on the flat mesa for less than a quarter mile before heading down a 1,000-foot descent into Murphy Basin. Like other such descents from Island in the Sky, the NPS has expertly routed and contoured the trail to make it safe and enjoyable walking. In one place a wooden bridge was installed to securely cross a short steep spot.

25 Murphy Basin; 26 Murphy Point

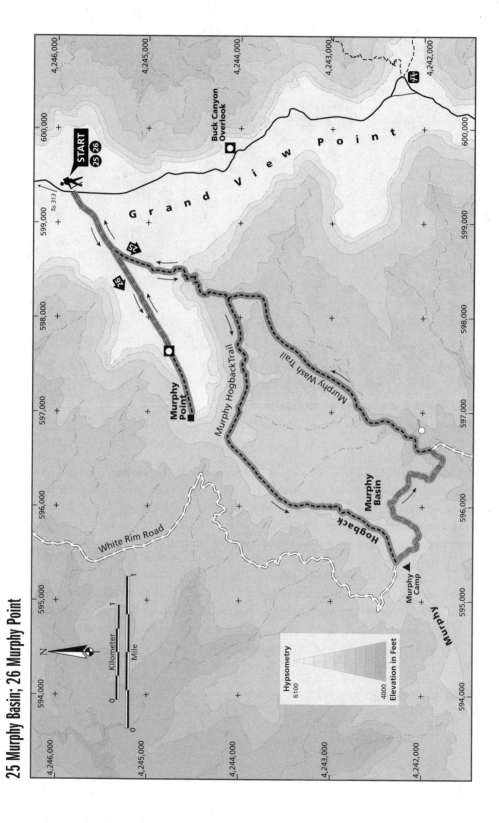

Looking down into Murphy Basin.

Right at the bottom of the mile-long descent the trail splits, with the right fork following the hogback and the left fork dropping into the dry wash. Take your pick on which way you want to do the 7-mile loop section of this trail. If you go right you follow a flat, well-defined, packed dirt trail all the way to White Rim Road. The trail stays on a small mesa and makes for pleasant walking.

When you reach White Rim Road, take a left (south). You'll see Murphy Vehicle Campsite and a vault toilet. Continue down White Rim Road for about 1.3 miles until you see the sign for the Murphy Wash Trail, which heads up the dry wash. The trail stays in the dry wash until just before the big climb back up to Island in the Sky. The climb looks even more daunting from below than it did from above. The cliff looks like sheer rock with no possibility of a safe trail, but at the top you'll probably say something to the effect that it wasn't half as hard as it looked.

Miles and Directions

0.5 End of abandoned road.

1.5 Junction with Murphy Wash Trail, turn right.

4.5	White Rim Road, turn left.
4.8	Murphy Vehicle Campsite.
5.8	Junction with Murphy Wash Trail, turn left.
8.5	Junction with Murphy Hogback Trail, turn right.
9.5	Abandoned road.
10.0	Murphy Trailhead.

26 Murphy Point

Start: Murphy Trailhead.
Distance: 4 miles.
Type of hike: Day hike, out-and-back.
Difficulty: Easy.
Maps: Trails Illustrated Island in the Sky and USGS Monument Basin and Turks Head.

Trail contact: Canyonlands National Park, 2282 South West Resource Boulevard, Moab, UT 84532; (435) 719-2313; www.nps.gov/cany.

Finding the trailhead: (See map on page 89.) Drive 8.6 miles south from the Island in the Sky Visitor Center and park at the pullout at the Murphy Trailhead.

The Hike

The Murphy Point Trail used to be Murphy Point Road, which went to within 0.2 mile of the overlook. In 1996 the NPS converted the road to a trail starting at the Murphy Trailhead. (Some older maps may still show it as a road.) This created a nice 2-mile hike with an absolutely stunning view.

The trail is mostly flat as it stays on the same level as Island in the Sky. Because you're walking on what used to be a two-wheel-drive road, it's easy going. About 0.2 mile from the point, the trail reaches the spot where vehicles used to park. The rest of the way is on an easy trail with some slickrock sections.

From the point you get a breathtaking view of the White Rim Country west of Island in the Sky, including the Green River slowly making its way to a grand meeting with the Colorado River a few miles later. Junction Butte dominates the southern horizon. You can see White Rim Road curving along the White Rim Sandstone far below. Plan on spending some extra time here relaxing and soaking in the incredible expansiveness of the canyonlands.

You actually can spend the night on Murphy Point. The NPS has recently designated a backcountry campsite in the area. Ask about it at the visitor center. If a permit is available, you can park your vehicle at the Murphy Trailhead and hike about a mile into the Murphy Point area and spend the night.

27 Gooseberry

Start: Island in the Sky Picnic Area.
Distance: 6 miles.
Type of hike: Day hike, out-and-back.
Difficulty: Strenuous.
Maps: Trails Illustrated Island in the Sky and USGS Monument Basin.

Trail contact: Canyonlands National Park, 2282 South West Resource Boulevard, Moab, UT 84532; (435) 719-2313; www.nps.gov/cany.

Finding the trailhead: (See map on page 93.) Drive 11.2 miles south from the Island in the Sky Visitor Center and turn left (east) into the picnic area. There is no trailhead sign on the main road.

The Hike

When you look over the edge of Island in the Sky at the top of the Gooseberry Trail, it looks like you're getting ready to jump off a cliff. At this point it's tempting

The daunting start of the Gooseberry Trail.

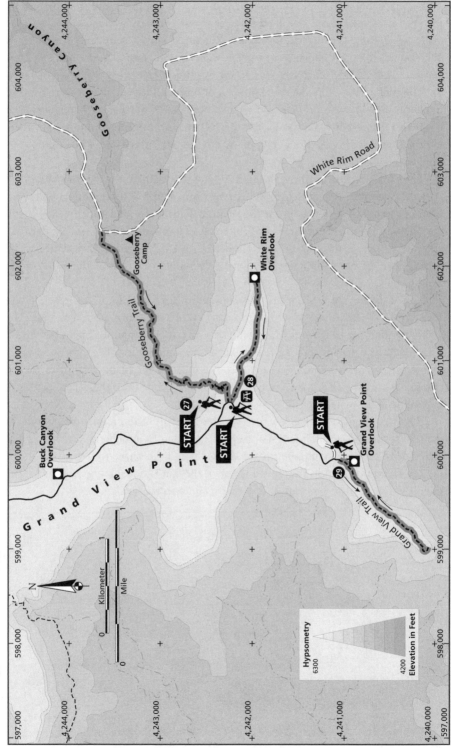

to turn back, but you might be sorry if you do. This is a great hike. It is perfect for the person who has been confined to a car for several days of sightseeing and now really needs some serious cardiovascular exercise. If you're a nontechnical climber, you can also hike this trail and then tell everybody you climbed to Island in the Sky because that's exactly what you will do on this hike.

The trail drops 1,400 feet over the span of 3 miles. That might not seem too bad until you look at the topo map and see that you lose 1,300 feet of that elevation in less than 1.5 miles. It looks deadly, but the NPS has done a superb job of constructing the trail to minimize the climb and make it as safe as possible. With a little caution, it's very safe.

The trail switchbacks down the steep side of the Island in the Sky formation and then drops into the dry wash for Gooseberry Canyon. While descending, watch your footing carefully—you can slip in the sections with loose sand. On the way down the hill, you get excellent views of White Rim Country, and you can see the road ahead—perhaps with ant-size vehicles driving on it. In spring the white of the snowcapped La Sal Mountains merges nicely with the white of the White Rim Sandstone.

Once in the dry wash, it's easy hiking and nearly level until you reach White Rim Road. When you get down to the road, you have to turn around and face the reality of climbing back up to the picnic area. It can be a daunting sight, but, again, it isn't that bad for anybody in reasonable physical condition. Take it slowly, make frequent rest stops to check out the scenery, and you might find it just as easy as coming down. The trail is the steepest in the last 0.5 mile from the top, but still safe with all its little switchbacks.

When coming back up the arroyo for the first half of the return trip, watch for the trail to take a sharp left and stair step up the side of Gooseberry Canyon. If you aren't alert you could continue up the dry wash and then have to backtrack.

Try to do this hike in the morning when the sun is not shining directly on the trail. If you start early, you can do the entire climb in the shade.

28 White Rim Overlook

Start: Island in the Sky Picnic Area.
Distance: 1.5 miles.
Type of hike: Day hike, out-and-back.
Difficulty: Easy.
Maps: Trails Illustrated Island in the Sky and USGS Monument Basin.

Trail contact: Canyonlands National Park, 2282 South West Resource Boulevard, Moab, UT 84532; (435) 719-2313; www.nps.gov/cany.

Finding the trailhead: (See map on page 93.) Drive 11.2 miles south from the Island in the Sky Visitor Center and turn left (east) into the picnic area. There is no trailhead sign on the main road.

The view from White Rim Overlook.

The Hike

You can get a good view of the White Rim area from the parking lot, but a short enjoyable walk gives you a really good view. The White Rim Overlook Trail starts at the right (south) side of the parking lot. It's flat and easy to follow the entire way. Some sections rely on well-placed cairns to show the way.

The trail ends at the end of a peninsula jutting out to the east from the Island in the Sky mesa. From the end of the trail, you can soak in an incredible panoramic view of the entire area. If it's near lunchtime, bring along a snack and a drink and have your lunch surrounded by the quiet beauty of the high desert before heading back to the parking lot.

29 Grand View

Start: Grand View Point Overlook.
Distance: 2 miles.
Type of hike: Day hike, out-and-back.
Difficulty: Easy.

Maps: Trails Illustrated Island in the Sky and USGS Monument Basin.
Trail contact: Canyonlands National Park, 2282 South West Resource Boulevard, Moab, UT 84532; (435) 719-2313; www.nps.gov/cany.

Finding the trailhead: (See map on page 93.) Drive south from the Island in the Sky Visitor Center for 12 miles all the way to the end of the main road.

The Hike

The NPS has placed several wonderful interpretive signs at the Grand View Trailhead, including a panoramic sign that names many of the prominent features in the area such as the Totem Pole, the confluence of the Colorado and Green Rivers, and the White Rim Road winding its way around Island in the Sky.

This trail is flat all the way, but it's poorly defined in spots. There are lots of cairns, but some are small. Be careful not to get too close to the cliffs: It's a long way down. If you have small children, watch them carefully.

At the end of the trail, you can sit and absorb a grand view, contemplating how nature transformed what was formerly a featureless plain into what you see today.

30 Fort Bottom

Start: Fort Bottom Trailhead.
Distance: 2 miles to the ruin; 3 miles to the cabin.
Type of hike: Day hike, out-and-back.
Difficulty: Moderate.

Maps: Trails Illustrated Island in the Sky and USGS Horsethief Canyon.
Trail contact: Canyonlands National Park, 2282 South West Resource Boulevard, Moab, UT 84532; (435) 719-2313; www.nps.gov/cany.

Finding the trailhead: (See map on page 98.) From the entrance station drive White Rim Road in your high-clearance, four-wheel-drive vehicle for 66.1 miles and park at the parking area on the left (west) side of the road. You can also reach the trailhead from the north, 6.1 miles from the park boundary, if you have a four-wheel-drive vehicle.

Hikers climb to Fort Bottom Butte.

Fort Bottom

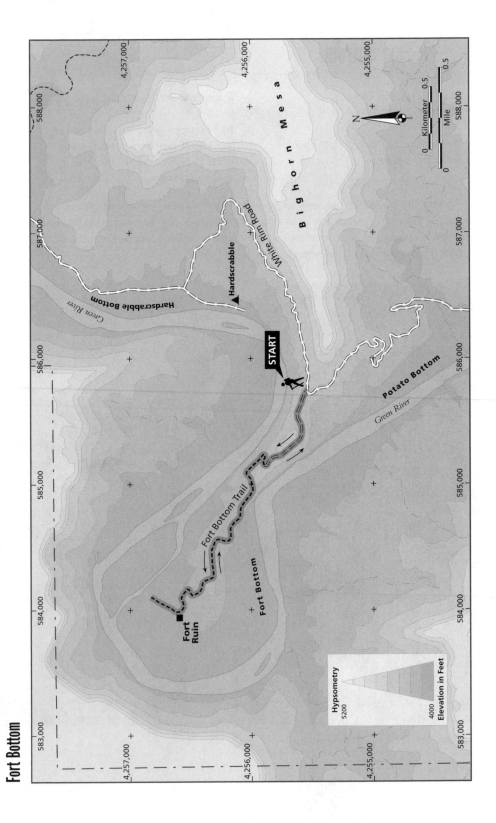

Tower structure atop Fort Bottom Butte.

The Hike

This is a very interesting hike with two different destinations. You can go down to the bottom where an old ranch building sits, or you can climb up to the top of a small butte to check out an intriguing structure built by ancestral Puebloans.

The first part of the trail is a recently abandoned road, so it's very easy walking. About a mile from the trailhead, you go over a little divide made out of bentonite clay and then around the north side of the butte. Once on the other side, you can take a left and go up to the ruin (which you could see on the way down), or right and go down to the bottom, the site of a historic ranching operation.

If you opt to climb up to the top of the butte, the trail gets a little rough for about 100 yards, including two little cliffs you need to climb, but you can safely do so. Once on top you can see the structure, but don't go in it or touch it. Tower structures are very common throughout the Southwest. This is the only known tower structure within Canyonlands National Park.

The trail down to the bottom is easier, so if you have children, this might be a better choice instead of climbing up to the top of the butte. The trail to the bottom is easy all the way. When you get down there, you can see one old cabin and an area where a recent fire has destroyed some majestic old cottonwoods. You can also take a pleasant nap on the bank of the Green River.

31 Gooseneck

Start: Gooseneck turnoff on White Rim Road.
Distance: 1 mile (round-trip).
Type of hike: Day hike, out-and-back.
Difficulty: Easy.

Maps: Trails Illustrated Island in the Sky and USGS Musselman Arch.
Trail contact: Canyonlands National Park, 2282 South West Resource Boulevard, Moab, UT 84532; (435) 719-2313; www.nps.gov/cany.

Finding the trailhead: (See map below.) From the entrance station, drive 6.4 miles on the White Rim Road and park at the parking area on the left (east) side of the road.

The Hike

At this point on White Rim Road, due east of the Island in the Sky Visitor Center, you'll have been bumping along on some of the rockiest sections of road, so a little hike might be just what you need. If so, the Gooseneck will be just right. This pleasant trail would be a great diversion from your mountain bike or four-wheeler.

This is a short walk, only about a half mile one-way. Take a snack and relax for a few moments at this very scenic overlook. You can see a huge sweeping meander in the Colorado River as it slowly heads south for its big meeting with the Green River just around the corner. You can also see a huge balanced rock right below the overlook, rivaling the famous balanced rock in Arches National Park. The trail is mostly on slickrock, but numerous cairns clearly show the way. It's a slightly uphill grade to the overlook.

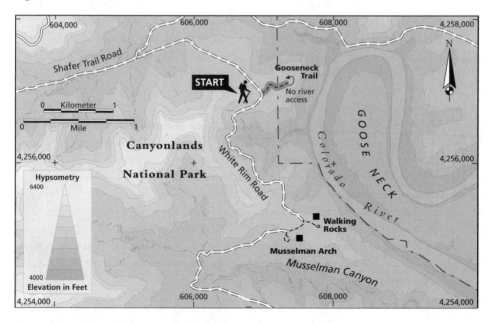

CANYONLANDS NATIONAL PARK:
The Needles

The Needles District of Canyonlands National Park is a high desert paradise. It is a jumbled landscape dominated by a series of distinctive sandstone spires called, of course, the Needles. Perhaps the other distinctive feature of the Needles District is an extensive trail system that offers nearly endless hiking options.

The Needles District has more hiking trails (about 55 miles) and a better variety of trails than the Island in the Sky or Maze Districts. In addition this area is, in general, set up and managed for hikers with lots of loop trails and a good selection of easy or moderate hiking options as well as long, multinight backpacking opportunities. Most trails have sections that go over slickrock, so get used to following cairns. In 1996 the NPS finished work on a designated backcountry campsite system.

The following pages include many suggested hikes, but the Needles District has so many trails and hiking options that you can easily get out the map and find additional options. Rangers at the Needles Visitor Center are most helpful in suggesting a hike that might be just right for you.

For mountain bikers and four-wheelers, the Needles District might not offer as much as the Maze or Island in the Sky Districts, but the area does have several backcountry roads. Some have well-placed scenic campsites, so visitors with four-wheel-drive vehicles can base camp and day hike from their backcountry vehicle camp.

The Needles District has a great visitor center about a quarter mile past the entrance station. The Squaw Flat Campground has twenty-six campsites with picnic tables, pit toilets, fire rings (bring your own wood), and a water supply (spring through fall). The campsites go on a first-come, first-served basis, and you'll be lucky to get one during peak seasons. The Needles District also has three group sites, which can be reserved in advance. Both individual sites in the campground and group sites have nominal fees.

The Needles District has more water than other sections of Canyonlands National Park or Arches National Park. In spring you can often find a flowing stream in several canyons. However, be sure to carry your own water instead of depending

Diverse vegetation surrounds a spring along the Upper Salt Creek Trail.

on unreliable desert water sources. Also in spring, the entire area can be awash with wildflowers.

From Moab, take U.S. Highway 191 south for 40 miles and turn right (west) onto Highway 211. Follow this paved road 35 miles to the Needles District Entrance Station. Be careful not to take Needles Overlook Road, which takes off a few miles before the correct junction. This road does not take you to Canyonlands National Park. Watch for the CANYONLANDS NATIONAL PARK sign before turning. From Monticello drive 14 miles north on US 191 and turn left (west) onto Highway 211.

HIKING AT NIGHT CAN BE A REAL DRAG

The Needles District attracts thousands of hikers, some of whom are inexperienced. One fairly common—and serious—problem is that less-experienced hikers underestimate how much time it takes to complete a hike. Then they get caught by nightfall and, in many cases, without a flashlight or headlamp.

Even with a flashlight or headlamp, following Needles trails at night can be very challenging. Most trails have slickrock sections and go along canyon washes, making it easy to miss a cairn and get off the trail. Be extra careful not to underestimate the time a hike will take or overestimate your physical abilities—especially when summer heat can significantly slow you down.

32 Roadside Ruin

Start: Roadside Ruin Parking Area.
Distance: 0.3 mile.
Type of hike: Short day hike, loop.
Difficulty: Easy.

Maps: Trails Illustrated Needles and USGS The Loop.
Trail contact: Canyonlands National Park, 2282 South West Resource Boulevard, Moab, UT 84532; (435) 719-2313; www.nps.gov/cany.

Finding the trailhead: (See map on page 105.) Drive 0.6 mile from the Needles Entrance Station and park on the south side of the road in the well-signed Roadside Ruin Parking Area.

The Hike

This hike offers an easy introduction to the Canyonlands and its cultural history and plant life. At the trailhead you can spend a quarter and get a brochure for this self-guided trail. The trail is well defined and easy walking all the way.

Along the short, flat route, signs identify key native plant species, and the brochure describes these plants and how American Indians used them. At the end of the loop, you can see a granary typical of the structures found throughout the park, although few are as well preserved as this one.

33 Cave Spring

Start: Cave Spring Parking Area.
Distance: 0.6 mile.
Type of hike: Short day hike, loop.
Difficulty: Moderate.

Maps: Trails Illustrated Needles and USGS The Loop.
Trail contact: Canyonlands National Park, 2282 South West Resource Boulevard, Moab, UT 84532; (435) 719-2313; www.nps.gov/cany.

Finding the trailhead: (See map on page 105.) Drive 0.9 mile west from the Needles Entrance Station, take a left (south) onto a paved road (sign points to Salt Creek), and go 0.5 mile before taking another left (east) onto a dirt road. The unpaved road ends in 1.2 miles at the parking area and trailhead for the Cave Spring Trail.

The Hike

If you're in the Needles area and have an extra hour, the Cave Spring hike would be an easy and pleasant way to spend it. The trailhead is conveniently located, and this short hike offers lots of diversity. You can pick up a brochure that explains the area's history and plant life at the trailhead.

32 Roadside Ruin; 33 Cave Spring

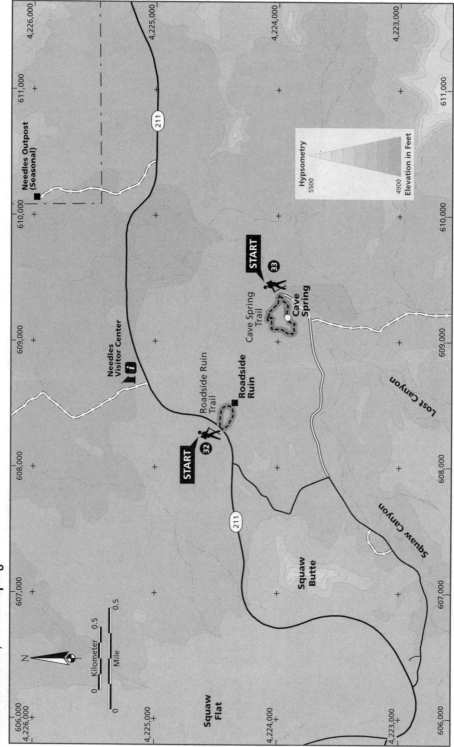

The small loop trail goes by ruins of historic ranching operations that were active here until 1975, when grazing was abandoned in Canyonlands National Park. Please honor the barriers put up by the NPS to preserve this part of the area's history. Later the trail goes by Cave Spring and then passes by some rock art left by the ancestral Puebloans who inhabited the area 1,000 years ago. Please don't touch these rock-art treasures.

After you finish enjoying the signs of both recent and ancient history, hike around a large "Canyonlands mushroom" and climb a safety ladder to a slickrock flat. Here you get the experience of following cairns over slickrock and also get a great view of many of the area's main features such as the Needles, North Six-shooter Peak, and South Six-shooter Peak.

34 Pothole Point

Start: Pothole Point Parking Area.
Distance: 0.6 mile.
Type of hike: Short day hike, loop.
Difficulty: Easy.

Maps: Trails Illustrated Needles and USGS The Loop.
Trail contact: Canyonlands National Park, 2282 South West Resource Boulevard, Moab, UT 84532; (435) 719-2313; www.nps.gov/cany.

Finding the trailhead: (See map on page 108.) From the Needles Entrance Station, drive 5.1 miles and park on the left (west) side of the road in the Pothole Point Parking Area.

The Hike

If you need a little exercise or want to take small children for an easy, safe hike where they might learn something about desert ecology, Pothole Point is an excellent choice. For a quarter you can buy a small brochure at the trailhead. The brochure explains the fascinating ecology of potholes.

Most of this hike follows a string of cairns over slickrock. The name Pothole Point comes from the numerous "potholes" that have formed in the slickrock along most of the trail. Once started, a pothole traps water after a desert rain. The rainwater is mildly acidic and ever so slowly enlarges the pothole. An intricate, symbiotic animal community featuring shrimp, worms, snails, and perhaps even a Great Basin spadefoot toad gradually develops in some potholes. If you're lucky enough to visit Pothole Point shortly after a rain, you can observe these tiny ecosystems.

Over time the wind continuously blows dirt, sand, and small bits of organic material into the potholes. Eventually plants take root in the thin layer of soil. The

◀ *A ladder on the Cave Spring Trail.*

34 Pothole Point; 35 Slickrock Foot Trail; 36 Confluence Overlook

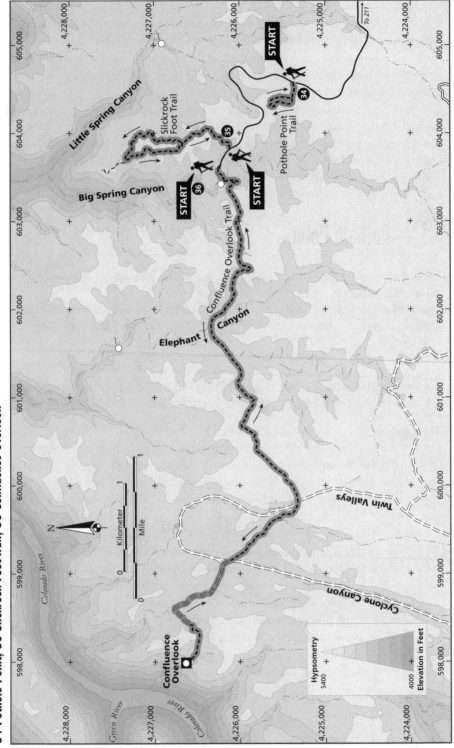

first sign of life in a pothole is often the cryptobiotic soil, which provides the foundation for growth of larger plants. The end result is a "pothole garden," a pocket of miniature, bonsai-like vegetation in a bowl of solid rock.

You can hike this short loop in either direction. Watch for a spur trail going to the top of some big boulders where you can get a great view of the surrounding terrain in either direction, including the area's namesake, the Needles.

35 Slickrock Foot Trail

Start: Slickrock Foot Trail Parking Area.
Distance: 2.4 miles.
Type of hike: Day hike, loop (actually a "lollipop").
Difficulty: Moderate.

Maps: Trails Illustrated Needles and USGS The Loop.
Trail contact: Canyonlands National Park, 2282 South West Resource Boulevard, Moab, UT 84532; (435) 719-2313; www.nps.gov/cany.

Finding the trailhead: (See map on page 108.) From the Needles Entrance Station, drive 6.4 miles and park on the right (north) side of the road at the Slickrock Foot Trail Parking Area, just before the end of the road.

The Hike

If you're a beginning or experienced hiker with only a half-day to spend in the Needles District, the Slickrock Foot Trail is an excellent way to enjoy it. Many hikes in the Needles follow canyon bottoms, but this trail stays high and gives an overall perspective of the entire southeastern corner of Canyonlands National Park.

The NPS suggests this trail to inexperienced hikers so that they can get a look at the entire area before deciding where they want to go on their next trip. On this trail, beginners also learn how to follow cairns and hike on slickrock. For the beginner who has only walked well-defined dirt trails, this hike might be a little adventuresome, but it certainly isn't dangerous. The trail is easy to follow with lots of cairns marking the way. Well-placed signs mark the way to four viewpoints and the point where the loop begins.

Spend a quarter at the trailhead on a handy brochure written for this hike. It describes much of the geology of the area and is keyed specifically to the four viewpoints along the trail.

Take the hike counterclockwise as indicated by a NPS sign about a half mile up the trail where the loop section of the trail begins. Viewpoint No. 1 occurs just before you get to the start of the loop. At this viewpoint you get a nice panoramic view of the entire region and many of the major landmarks—Six-shooter Peak, Elaterite Butte, Cathedral Butte, the La Sal Mountains, Ekker Butte, and, of course, the Needles.

The trail stays on the ridge between Little Spring Canyon and Big Spring Canyon. At Viewpoint No. 2 you can get a good view into the upper reaches of Little Spring Canyon.

After Viewpoint No. 3 the trail turns west and then south. You can take a long look at the region's namesake, the Needles, as you walk along.

Finding Viewpoint No. 4 is more difficult and time-consuming than the first three. It's about a quarter mile walk to this viewpoint, whereas the first three were only 50 to 100 feet off the trail. At Viewpoint No. 4 you can look down into massive Big Spring Canyon. In spring you can see a stream flowing in the distance far below. The brochure gives you a great geology lesson from this viewpoint, so plan on spending extra time here to identify all the different strata that make up the canyon's awesome cliffs.

After leaving Viewpoint No. 4, it's another mile or so back to the trailhead, most of the trail following the east flank of Big Spring Canyon.

36 Confluence Overlook

Start: Parking area at end of main park road at the Big Spring Canyon Overlook.
Distance: 11 miles.
Type of hike: Long day hike, out-and-back.
Difficulty: Strenuous.

Maps: Trails Illustrated Needles and USGS The Loop and Spanish Bottom.
Trail contact: Canyonlands National Park, 2282 South West Resource Boulevard, Moab, UT 84532; (435) 719-2313; www.nps.gov/cany.

Finding the trailhead: (See map on page 108.) From the Needles Entrance Station, drive 6.6 miles and park at the end of the road.

The Hike

This is a serious hike, but the destination—a sweeping vista of the confluence of two great rivers—makes up for any discomfort in getting there. Some sections go over slickrock marked with strings of cairns, but unlike most trails in the Canyonlands, most of this trail is a well-defined dirt path. The NPS has expertly routed the trail through many interesting features, taking advantage of the great scenery along the way. Immediately after leaving the trailhead, the trail drops steeply into Big Spring Canyon. Then, after about 25 feet in the dry wash, the trail climbs the other side of the canyon. Be careful not to take the well-used off-trail route up the canyon and miss the cairns going off to the right, marking the ascent out of the canyon.

The climb is well marked with cairns, but footing can be a bit precarious in a few places. In one spot the NPS has installed a safety ladder. Once on top take a break in a gorgeous spot where the trail goes through a small opening between two cliffs. Looking either way through this little "keyhole" gives you a great photo.

The Confluence Overlook Trail in the Needles District goes through a narrow "keyhole" before dropping into Elephant Canyon, a great place for a rest and to enjoy the high desert scenery.

After leaving the keyhole you stay high for about a mile. Here you can see some well-sculpted and huge "Canyonlands mushrooms" before gradually dropping into expansive Elephant Canyon. Once down in Elephant Canyon, you follow a dry wash for about a mile, all easy walking. Then you start a gradual climb out of Elephant Canyon—going by a giant red sandstone spire with no name and into another big and equally beautiful drainage called Twin Valleys. From above you can look out and see the "twins," which almost look cultivated with a light-colored grass carpeting the valley floor.

Just as you get into Twin Valleys, you cross a four-wheel-drive road that goes north and south. The trail goes right across the road and continues on. The flat bottomland of Twin Valleys is carpeted with cheatgrass, a nasty species brought into the area when it was heavily grazed (before the park was designated). Cheatgrass has completely taken over the area from native species, but its light-green color contrasts nicely with the other green hues of the high desert.

After leaving the gentle grasslands of Twin Valleys, you crest a small knoll and drop into Cyclone Canyon, also invaded with cheatgrass. In Cyclone Canyon you cross the four-wheel-drive road again. This time, however, the trail turns into a road.

Two mighty rivers, the Green and Colorado, merge below the overlook at the end of the Confluence Overlook Trail.

(Some maps show this as a trail, but on the ground it's a well-used road. Follow the road instead of looking around for the trail that isn't there.) Walk west 0.3 mile on the road, being careful not to take the north/south road through Cyclone Canyon. There are signs showing the way.

At the end of the road, you find a vault toilet, a picnic table, and another sign informing you that it's still another 0.5 mile to the Confluence Overlook. It's a gradual climb to the overlook from here.

The overlook is incredible. You can see two mighty rivers merging. The Colorado's namesake carries on, and the Green River ceases to exist, at least in name. You also can get a good panoramic view to the west and north into the Maze and Island in the Sky regions of the park with Ekker Butte highlighting the horizon. The overlook is unfenced, so don't get too close to the edge. If you have children, watch them carefully.

On the way back you'll notice that the NPS situated the parking lot in an appropriate location. You can see your vehicle from about a mile away as you come out of Elephant Canyon and head down into Big Spring Canyon.

Miles and Directions

1.2 Safety ladder.

1.5 Divide between Big Spring and Elephant Canyons.

4.2 Four-wheel-drive road.

4.7 Four-wheel-drive road.

5.0 End of road.

5.5 Confluence Overlook.

37 Upper Salt Creek

Start: For the shuttle hike, park outside the park at the Bureau of Land Management's Cathedral Butte Trailhead. For the out-and-back hike, park at the trailhead 1 mile before the end of Salt Creek Road.
Distance: 24.2 miles.
Type of hike: A backpacking adventure with several options, shuttle.

Difficulty: Strenuous.
Maps: Trails Illustrated Needles and USGS Druid Arch, South Six-shooter Peak, and Cathedral Butte.
Trail contact: Canyonlands National Park, 2282 South West Resource Boulevard, Moab, UT 84532; (435) 719–2313; www.nps.gov/cany.

Finding the trailhead: (See map on pages 116 and 117.) From the park entrance station, drive east out of the park on Highway 211 for 13.7 miles and turn right (south) onto a gravel road marked ELK MOUNTAIN AND BEEF BASIN. If you're coming from the east, the turnoff is 20 miles from US 191. Follow this well-maintained, unpaved road for 17 miles until you see the small parking area on your right (north) with a BLM sign that reads BRIGHT ANGEL AND SALT CREEK. This is officially called the Cathedral Butte Trailhead. There may be a gate across the road about 9.5 miles from Highway 211. You can open the gate and pass through, but be sure to close it behind you. You don't need a four-wheel-drive vehicle to get to the Cathedral Butte Trailhead unless it has rained recently, which can make the clay in the road very slippery. However, you do need a four-wheel-drive vehicle to get to the end of Salt Creek Road. If you plan to stay overnight in Salt Creek or Horse Canyon, be sure to get your overnight permit at the Needles Visitor Center. You also need a day-use permit for Salt Creek.

To find Salt Creek Backcountry Road, drive 0.9 mile west from the entrance station and take a left (south) onto a well-signed, paved road (marked SALT CREEK) and go 0.5 mile before taking a left (east) onto a two-wheel-drive unpaved road. About 0.5 mile up the unpaved road, turn right (south) instead of going straight to the Cave Spring Trailhead. Then go 0.5 mile more until you see a locked gate across the road. This gate marks the official trailhead for Salt Creek and Horse Canyon Roads.

The Hike

Names can be misleading. Somehow, "Salt Creek" seems to describe a dry, harsh, and unpleasant place when quite the opposite is true. Upper Salt Creek is definitely one

The Upper Salt Creek Trail winds through an unusually wide, flat high desert valley.

of the most delightful hikes in the Canyonlands region, and it deserves a name like "Paradise Creek."

First of all, unlike most "creeks" in the region, this one really is a creek. A stream flows through much of the canyon. Because of the reliable source of water, early cultures inhabited the area. Rock art and ruins can be found throughout the canyon.

Second, this is not the typical, narrow canyon common in Canyonlands. Instead it's a broad, flat, spacious valley with rich vegetative diversity ranging from cattail marshes to stately cottonwoods. And unlike many places in the park, Salt Creek has lots of wildlife—mule deer, coyote, bobcat, and even the mighty mountain lion. You might not see them, but you can see their tracks in the sand and mud.

Any way you look at it, the remoteness of Upper Salt Creek makes it a backpacking adventure. It's at least a three-day trip, and more like a four- or five-day trip for the out-and-back option.

You can hike into Upper Salt Creek and back from the end of Salt Creek Backcountry Road at Peekaboo Camp. However, the best way to see this hidden corner of Canyonlands is to arrange a shuttle. Start the hike at the south end and have somebody meet you or leave a vehicle at the north end where the trail meets Salt Creek Backcountry Road. This allows you to hike downhill all the way. If you did the shuttle route in reverse, it would be 24 miles uphill, with a very steep grade at the south end as you climb up to Cathedral Butte Trailhead.

If you can't arrange this time-consuming shuttle, you can still enjoy Upper Salt Creek by hiking out-and-back from Peekaboo Camp. However, it may be too long of a day hike to reach Upper Salt Creek and return in the same day. To get as far as Upper Jump, it's a 32-mile out-and-back hike, and you'd still miss the broad expansiveness of the southernmost reaches of Salt Creek.

Actually, you have one more option. If you have at least five days to spend in the wilderness, you can leave your vehicle at the Salt Creek gate and beg or bribe somebody to give you a ride to the Cathedral Butte Trailhead. You could continue hiking down Salt Creek Road past Peekaboo Camp for another 3.3 miles to the gate. At-large backpacking is allowed in Salt Creek Canyon (south and north of Peekaboo Camp) and Horse Canyon, and there are many attractive campsites. But make sure to get a permit and camp at least a mile from the road and away from any water sources.

After studying all the options, it's easy to see that the south-to-north shuttle is the best choice for this route. Getting a ride to the Cathedral Butte Trailhead might be problematic, but it's worth it. If you can't arrange for a pickup, you can have somebody leave a vehicle for you at the parking area near Peekaboo Camp, but not in the campsites. When you get your permit, the staff at the visitor center will tell you if the combination to the Salt Creek gate is scheduled to change while you're out hiking, so you don't fret about not being able to get out.

For a very fit and experienced hiker, the Upper Salt Creek shuttle hike could be done in one very long day, but to really enjoy "Paradise Creek," it's much better to plan on three or four days, as this trail description suggests.

Water is a big issue on such a long hike. Most of the time (but no guarantees) you can filter water out of Salt Creek. But storms and wind can make it too turbid to filter, so plan on always carrying emergency water, if for some reason you can't get more from the creek. Discuss this thorny issue with the visitor center staff when acquiring your backcountry permit.

The hike starts out in a juniper forest on a well-defined but rocky trail, which drops sharply for the first 1.5 miles. At the 1.5-mile mark, you'll see a big open canyon on your left, the upper reaches of Salt Creek. The rather indistinct Bright Angel Trail from the west joins the main trail after you drop into the valley. You might miss this unmarked junction, but it doesn't matter.

After walking through the open canyon for less than a quarter mile, you drop into the dry wash and see the park boundary signs. The NPS has put up signs on both sides of the dry wash so you won't miss them. The trail stays in the dry wash for about 100 yards before it veers left (west) at the second park boundary sign.

Upper Salt Creek

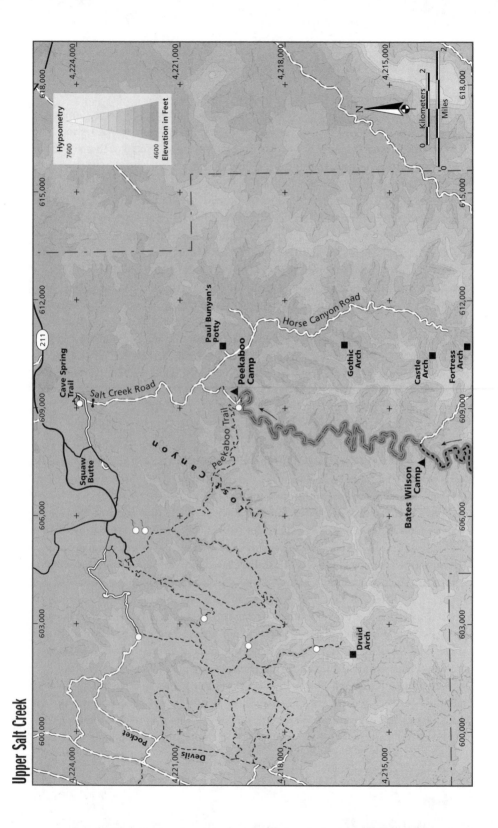

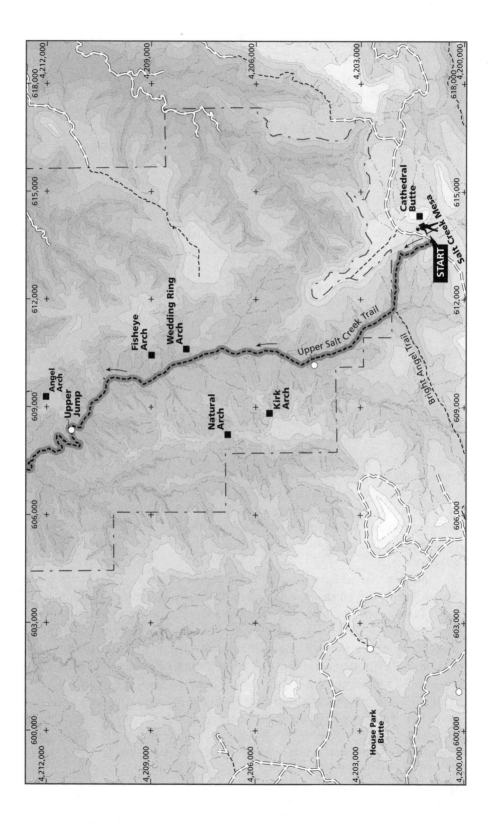

For the next 7 miles, the trail stays in the broad valley. It's a well-defined, packed dirt trail all the way. It occasionally gets brushy as it weaves around the sagebrush, saltbrush, and rabbitbrush. In addition to watching deer bound away, you can see four beautiful arches—Kirk and Natural on your left and Wedding Ring and Fisheye on your right. Kirk and Natural are on the skyline and easy to see, but only from a short section of trail, so be alert. Wedding Ring is right by the trail, but surprisingly easy to miss, so watch carefully. Fisheye is very obvious, standing out right in front of you.

At the 3.5-mile mark, the vegetation changes dramatically. A large spring in the area has created a series of cattail marshes and willow thickets and, in a few places, patches of green grass. After emerging from the thickets, the spring flows over some flat rocks as a full-blown stream, a great place to relax for a while. There is a large pool below the spring, but please resist the temptation to jump in. All the springs in Upper Salt Creek provide critical water supplies to wildlife and backpackers. You could contaminate them with skin oils, sunscreen, or soap. Park regulations prohibit bathing in any water sources except the Colorado and Green Rivers and in Salt Creek along the four-wheel-drive road. About a quarter mile beyond the spring, you'll see Kirk Cabin and the remains of a ranching operation that predates the creation of Canyonlands National Park. This aging cabin is part of the cultural history of the park, so be careful not to artificially increase the rate of deterioration, just as you would be careful not to harm any ancient ruins or rock art.

Shortly after Kirk Cabin the trail goes by the first backcountry campsites (SC1 and SC2) on the right (east) side of the trail. SC2 is about 100 yards from the trail nestled in a flat open spot in the sagebrush. SC1 is farther from the trail in a juniper stand and has a slightly better view. If you're on a two-night trip, one of these sites would be the best place to stop for the first night out.

After Kirk Cabin the trail continues to wind through the open valley floor. Keep your eyes peeled for arches in this section. About a mile after Fisheye Arch, the trail goes by a famous rock-art panel called All-American Man, perhaps because of its red, white, and blue pigments. Please don't climb up to the panel or touch this precious piece of art.

Right after All-American Man, the trail goes through a narrow spot between two cliffs. It's almost like going through an arch. This is a big departure from the last 5 miles of open valley, and it's a great place for a short rest and a good view of both where you've been and where you're going. Shortly after this tight spot, you go through a big thicket with a noticeably flowing Salt Creek, which stays that way for most of the rest of the hike. Near the end of the thicket, watch for Backcountry Campsite SC3 off to your left. This is a good choice for your second night out.

About a half mile past the thicket, the trail passes a delightful spot where the stream falls over a rock ledge and into a gorgeous pool. This is called Upper Jump, and it seems almost tropical and out of character for this neck of the woods. Again, please resist the temptation to jump into this critical water source.

Upper Jump.

After Upper Jump, the canyon walls gradually close in, and Upper Salt Creek starts to resemble many other canyons in the park. The trail also starts following the wide meanders of the stream. In fact, during the next 5 miles of the hike, the trail winds unmercifully. It seems to turn around every bush and crosses the stream dozens of times. The result is 5 miles of hiking to go about 2 miles "as the crow flies." This section of trail also goes through several stretches of very thick brush. If you don't have long pants on, you might end up looking like a poster child for Neosporin. It's worth it to stop and switch over to long pants.

In some places the trail stays on the bench above the stream, and in other places it goes right into the brushy stream bottom. When by the stream, it's nice and cool, and the trail is often carpeted with cottonwood leaves.

At the 12-mile mark, you'll see Backcountry Campsite SC4 on your right on a beautiful bench under some big cottonwoods, near the stream, and with a great view of a giant rock balanced on a sandstone spire. This is the last designated campsite. After going another 1.5 miles, you reach the point where Salt Creek Backcountry Road (and this hike) formerly ended. Now, however, it's another 10.7 miles to Peek-aboo Camp and the new terminus of Salt Creek Backcountry Road. This section is open to at-large camping, so you can find a suitable campsite for your last night anywhere along this section of road-turned-to-trail.

Before you head down the former road toward Peekaboo Camp, you might want to try a short (about 1 mile round-trip) side trip up to Angel Arch. The trail starts where the road used to end. The short, mostly level trail is easy to follow but sandy most of the way. It climbs slightly near the end up to a small ridge that becomes a great viewing platform for this magnificent arch. However, the trail doesn't go all the way to the arch.

As you hike this last nearly 11-mile section of the route, you might wonder why it was ever a road. The scenery is great, and in most cases the walking is fairly easy.

Miles and Directions

1.5 Canyonlands National Park boundary.

3.5 Kirk Cabin.

3.7 Backcountry Campsites SC1 and SC2.

7.5 All-American Man.

8.3 Backcountry Campsite SC3.

8.5 Upper Jump.

12.0 Backcountry Campsite SC4.

13.5 Start of the newly abandoned section of Salt Creek Backcountry Road, now part of Upper Salt Creek Trail, and trail to Angel Arch.

24.2 Start of Salt Creek Backcountry Road and Peekaboo Camp.

38 Castle Arch

Start: Castle Arch Trailhead near the end of Horse Canyon Road.
Distance: 0.8 mile.
Type of hike: Short day hike, out-and-back.
Difficulty: Easy.

Maps: Trails Illustrated Needles and USGS South Six-shooter Peak.
Trail contact: Canyonlands National Park, 2282 South West Resource Boulevard, Moab, UT 84532; (435) 719-2313; www.nps.gov/cany.

Finding the trailhead: (See map on page 122.) From the entrance station drive 0.9 mile and turn left (south) onto a paved road marked SALT CREEK. Follow this road for 0.5 mile and then turn left (east) onto a gravel road. Follow this as it turns right (south) and go another 1 mile to the gate at the entrance to Salt Creek Road. From here use the combination on your permit to open the gate and follow Salt Creek Road and then Horse Canyon Road to the trailhead.

The Hike

Just before the end of Horse Canyon Road, you see the trailhead sign for CASTLE ARCH TRAIL and a spot to pull off the main road. From here the trail heads west through a heavily vegetated valley.

This is a pleasant, slightly uphill hike. The trail is primitive and brushy in places, but nicely carpeted with oak leaves. It is a real treat for students of high desert vegetation. You can see the arch throughout most of the hike. However, the trail doesn't go to the arch, and in fact has no clearly definable end. Instead it just gets more and more faint, and you know when it's time to take one last look at the arch and head back to your vehicle.

If after you get back to your vehicle you're interested in more exercise, you can walk about a quarter mile down the road to the Fortress Arch Trailhead and see both arches.

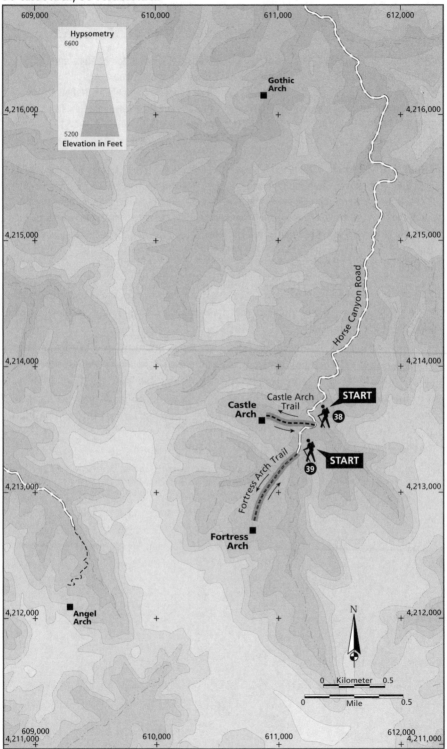

39 Fortress Arch

Start: Fortress Arch Trailhead at the end of the Horse Canyon Road.
Distance: 1 mile.
Type of hike: Short day hike, out-and-back.
Difficulty: Easy.

Maps: Trails Illustrated Needles and USGS South Six-shooter Peak.
Trail contact: Canyonlands National Park, 2282 South West Resource Boulevard, Moab, UT 84532; (435) 719-2313; www.nps.gov/cany.

Finding the trailhead: (See map on page 122.) From the entrance station drive 0.9 mile and turn left (south) onto a paved road marked SALT CREEK. Follow this road for 0.5 mile and then turn left (east) onto a gravel road. Follow this as it turns right (south) for another 1.5 miles to the gate at the entrance to Salt Creek Road. From here use the combination on your permit to open the gate and follow Salt Creek Road and then Horse Canyon to the trailhead at the end of Horse Canyon Road.

The Hike

The Fortress Arch Trail starts right at the end of Horse Canyon Road. From the parking area it heads up a dry wash and stays there most of the way. It's easy walking all the way. The trail ends near a big, flat rock that makes an excellent spot to relax for a few minutes while you view this massive arch.

40 Peekaboo

Start: Squaw Flat Trailhead.
Distance: 10 miles.
Type of hike: Long day hike or overnighter, out-and-back or shuttle.
Approximate hiking time: 6 to 8 hours.
Difficulty: Strenuous.

Maps: Trails Illustrated Needles and USGS The Loop and Druid Arch.
Trail contacts: Canyonlands National Park, 2282 South West Resource Boulevard, Moab, UT 84532; (435) 719-2313; www.nps.gov/cany.

Finding the trailhead: (See map on page 125.) Drive about 2.7 miles west from the Needles Entrance Station and turn left into Squaw Flat Campground. After entering the campground area, the road forks. Both forks go to trailheads with access to the same trails. However, the left-hand fork takes you to the trailhead with the shortest access route to the backcountry. Mostly campers staying in the campground use the right-hand fork and its respective trailhead.

The Hike

You have several options for seeing the Peekaboo Spring area. If you are in the mood for a long, strenuous day hike, it's 10 miles out-and-back. However, Salt

The Peekaboo Trail actually passes through a small, unnamed arch.

Creek Backcountry Road ends at Peekaboo Camp, so you can have less ambitious members of your party meet you there for a quiet night in a beautiful desert campsite—if you can get a permit for this popular vehicle campsite. You can also make this an overnighter by camping at Backcountry Campsite LC1 in Lost Canyon.

Immediately after leaving the trailhead, you reach the junction with the Big Spring Canyon Trail. Take a left here and head southeast toward Squaw Canyon. The first 1.1 miles of the trail are flat and easy, with the exception of several slickrock sections. The slickrock isn't dangerous, but be alert for small cairns marking the correct route. After 1.1 miles you hit another junction, also well signed. Take the left (east) fork toward Lost Canyon and Peekaboo Spring.

The next 1.5-mile section is gorgeous. It goes over slickrock for much of the first mile or so. Then, just after climbing down a small ladder, the trail follows the north rim of a beautiful, narrow canyon for a while before dropping into the sandy bottom of the canyon for the last half mile or so to the junction with the Lost Canyon Trail. If you're staying overnight, LC1 Backcountry Campsite is less than a quarter mile up the Peekaboo Trail on your right (south).

40 Peekaboo; 41 Lost Canyon

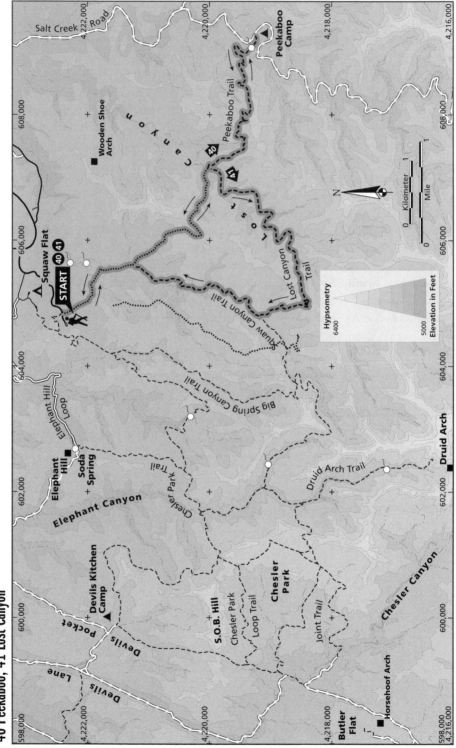

The Lost Canyon Trail junction is right in the dry wash of Lost Canyon. Go straight (east) across the wash instead of turning right (southwest) up Lost Canyon. Right after this junction, you quickly gain about 300 feet in elevation. This part of the hike is a bit rugged but very scenic. In spring the newly emerging leaves of the deciduous trees (oaks, cottonwoods, and willows) contrast nicely with the red and white sandstone formations in this area. Also, you're up on a ridgeline, so you can get great vistas in all directions. Near the end of the trail, you go right through a small arch and several other small arches are visible. Don't get too distracted by the scenery, though. You have to follow cairns most of the rest of the way to Peekaboo Camp.

Just before the end of the trail, you lose the elevation you gained coming out of Lost Canyon. It's steeper at the east end, and one spot could be dangerous if you aren't cautious. Fortunately, the NPS has installed a safety ladder to help you through this spot. After this steep section it's about a quarter mile on a well-defined, flat trail along the streambed of Salt Creek to Peekaboo Camp, which is nicely located under some stately old cottonwoods. After relaxing here for a while or staying overnight, retrace your steps to Squaw Flat Trailhead. While walking along Salt Creek (which often is flowing), be careful not to miss the trail when it takes a sharp left up a crack in the rock to reach the ladder you climbed down on your way to Peekaboo Camp.

Miles and Directions

0.1 Junction with Squaw Canyon Trail, turn left.

1.1 Junction with Peekaboo Trail, turn left.

2.6 Junction with Lost Canyon Trail, go straight.

5.0 Peekaboo Camp.

41 Lost Canyon

Start: Squaw Flat Trailhead.
Distance: 8.7 miles.
Type of hike: Long day hike or overnighter, loop (actually a "lollipop").
Difficulty: Moderate.

Maps: Trails Illustrated Needles and USGS The Loop and Druid Arch.
Trail contact: Canyonlands National Park, 2282 South West Resource Boulevard, Moab, UT 84532; (435) 719-2313; www.nps.gov/cany.

Finding the trailhead: (See map on page 125.) Drive about 2.7 miles west from the Needles Entrance Station and turn left into Squaw Flat Campground. After entering the campground area, the road forks. Both forks go to trailheads with access to the same trails. However, the left-hand fork takes you to the trailhead with the shortest access route to the backcountry. Mostly campers staying in the campground use the right-hand fork and its respective trailhead.

The Hike

Lost Canyon is well named. It's not only the kind of place you could get lost in, it's so beautiful that it is the kind of place you would like to get lost in. Like other loops, Lost Canyon can be done in either direction. This trail description describes the clockwise route.

The first 1.1 miles of the trail are flat and easy with several slickrock sections. The slickrock isn't dangerous, but don't miss the sometimes small cairns that mark the correct route. The sandstone formations on the horizon along this section are marvelous. After the first 1.1 miles of easy hiking, you reach the junction with the Peekaboo Trail. Take a left (east) and head toward Lost Canyon and Peekaboo Spring.

The next 1.5-mile section is mostly slickrock. Just after climbing down a small ladder, the trail follows the north rim of a beautiful, narrow canyon for a short way before dropping into the canyon on a sandy trail for the last 0.5 mile to the junction with the Lost Canyon Trail, which lies right in the dry wash of Lost Canyon. Take a right (southwest) here and start hiking up Lost Canyon. In spring a healthy stream often flows through this lush canyon. If you're lucky enough to hike this after a rain, you might actually get your feet wet, because the trail frequently crosses the streambed. But please don't wade in the water any more than necessary to cross the stream.

Lost Canyon starts out broad and flat but gets narrow in places later on. The vegetation is more diverse than most other canyons in the area (to the point of getting brushy in a few spots), and there are no slickrock sections. The multihued vegetation contrasts beautifully with the reddish sandstone to create some fantastic scenery.

In springtime a live stream often follows the trail through Lost Canyon.

If you plan to stay overnight, Lost Canyon has three designated campsites. The first is on your right (south) just a few yards down the Peekaboo Trail. The second one is about a mile up the trail on your right. The third site is on your right just as you start up a drainage back toward Squaw Canyon.

After hiking through Lost Canyon for about 2 miles, start watching carefully for a sharp turn to the right. There is a sign (pointing to LOST CANYON TRAIL), but if you're preoccupied with the scenery, you might miss it. An off-trail route continues up Lost Canyon, but at this point the official trail leaves Lost Canyon and dips into a narrow, unnamed canyon that runs north to south. If you have extra time, you can take note of this spot and then explore the upper reaches of Lost Canyon before heading back to the trailhead.

This slender, unnamed tributary is like a miniature Lost Canyon—smaller but perhaps even more beautiful. After following the dry wash of the narrow gorge for about a half mile, the trail climbs a steep chute (partly on an NPS-installed ladder) to a slickrock ledge. After cautiously hiking the ledge, you climb over a ridge. You then follow a trail of cairns over slickrock for another half mile or so until you drop into Squaw Canyon. This section can be hazardous, so be careful, especially if you have children along. A trail junction is just after you cross the dry wash of Squaw Canyon. Turn right at this junction.

If you didn't make your overnight stay in Lost Canyon, you have two more choices in Squaw Canyon. One site is on your left just before the junction with the Squaw Canyon Trail, and the second is on your left just less than 1 mile down the trail.

After hiking down Squaw Canyon for 1.7 miles, you hit the Peekaboo Trail again, where you turn left and retrace your steps 1.1 miles back to the Squaw Flat Trailhead.

Miles and Directions

0.1 Junction with Squaw Canyon Trail, turn left.

1.1 Junction with Peekaboo Trail, turn left.

2.6 Junction with Lost Canyon Trail, turn right.

2.7 LC1 Backcountry Campsite.

3.8 LC2 Backcountry Campsite.

5.2 LC3 Backcountry Campsite.

5.4 Sharp right (south) turn onto Lost Canyon Trail.

5.7 SQ2 Backcountry Campsite.

5.9 Junction with Squaw Canyon Trail, turn right.

6.7 SQ1 Backcountry Campsite.

7.6 Junction with Peekaboo Trail, turn left.

8.7 Squaw Flat Trailhead.

42 Lost Canyon/Elephant Canyon

Start: Squaw Flat Trailhead.
Distance: 13.8 miles.
Type of hike: Long day hike or short backpacking trip (one or two nights), loop.
Difficulty: Moderate (strenuous as a day hike).

Maps: Trails Illustrated Needles and USGS The Loop and Druid Arch.
Trail contact: Canyonlands National Park, 2282 South West Resource Boulevard, Moab, UT 84532; (435) 719-2313; www.nps.gov/cany.

Finding the trailhead: (See map on page 131.) Drive about 2.7 miles west from the Needles Entrance Station and turn left into Squaw Flat Campground. After entering the campground area, the road forks. Both forks go to trailheads with access to the same trails. However, the left-hand fork takes you to the trailhead with the shortest access route to the backcountry. Mostly campers staying in the campground use the right-hand fork and its respective trailhead.

The Hike

If you can afford the time to make this a three-day trip, you will have the opportunity to see most of the outstanding features of the Needles area. A three-day trip provides the time for side trips to Peekaboo, Upper Lost Canyon, and Druid Arch without your overnight pack.

This trail is described from a clockwise direction. It can, however, be done quite pleasantly in either direction. In either case, be sure to take plenty of water and flashlights just in case you get caught out at night.

The first 1.1 miles of this hike follow a flat and easy stretch of trail with several slickrock sections. Be alert not to miss the sometimes small cairns marking the correct route over the slickrock. After the first 1.1 miles of easy hiking, you reach the junction with the Peekaboo Trail. Take a left (east) and head toward Lost Canyon and Peekaboo Spring. Most of the next 1.5-mile section is on slickrock. After climbing down a small ladder, the trail follows the north rim of a beautiful, narrow canyon for a short way before dropping into the canyon on a sandy trail for the last 0.5 mile to the junction with the Lost Canyon Trail. Take a right (southwest) here and start hiking up Lost Canyon. In spring a healthy stream often flows through this lush canyon.

Lost Canyon starts out broad and flat but gets narrow in places later on. It has more diverse vegetative growth than most canyons in the area. In a few spots it actually gets brushy. The multihued vegetation of Lost Canyon contrasts beautifully with the reddish sandstone to create some fantastic scenery.

If you're spending two nights out, you might want to camp at LC1 or LC2 for your first night out. If you pick LC1 (on your right just past the Lost Canyon junction at the 2.7-mile mark), you can set up camp and then conveniently hike over to

42 Lost Canyon/Elephant Canyon; 43 Squaw Canyon/Big Spring Canyon

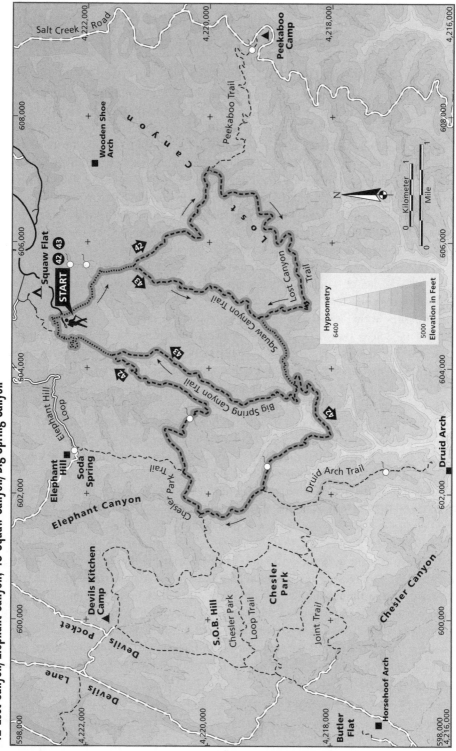

Peekaboo Spring and return to camp. You can also continue on to stay at LC2 (3.8-mile mark) or LC3 (5.2-mile mark). If you choose LC3, you are conveniently located to spend your extra time exploring the upper reaches of Lost Canyon and then return to camp.

After hiking through Lost Canyon for about 2 miles, start watching carefully for an abrupt right-hand turn in the trail. There is a sign (pointing to LOST CANYON TRAIL), but if you're absorbed in the scenery, you might miss it. An off-trail route continues up Lost Canyon, but at this point the official trail leaves Lost Canyon and dips into a narrow, unnamed canyon that runs north to south. This small tributary is like a miniature Lost Canyon—smaller, but perhaps even more beautiful. After following the dry wash of the narrow gorge for about a half mile, the trail climbs a steep chute to a slickrock ledge. After cautiously hiking the ledge, you climb over the ridge, then follow a trail of cairns over slickrock for another half mile or so until you drop into Squaw Canyon. This section can be hazardous, so be careful. A trail junction is just after you cross the dry wash of Squaw Canyon.

Just before you reach the Squaw Canyon Trail, watch for Backcountry Campsite SQ2 on your left (5.7-mile mark). If you're only taking two days for this trip, this is probably your best choice for your overnight stay. However, staying out only one night results in two tough days and limits free time for side trips.

At the Squaw Canyon Trail junction, take a left and head southwest up Squaw Canyon. The trail quickly angles off to the right out of the canyon bottom onto slickrock. It stays on slickrock for most of the next 0.9-mile section to the junction with the Big Spring Canyon Trail. Take another left at this junction, continuing southwesterly, again mostly on slickrock, for 2.1 miles to the Druid Arch Trail. This is an especially scenic section of trail, and in one spot you climb over a slickrock pass with the help of a ladder on each side of a joint in the rocks.

Look for the sign at the end of this section of trail right in the dry wash of Upper Elephant Canyon. If you're staying two nights, you probably want to spend the second night at UE1 (on your right just south of the Druid Arch Trail at the 9-mile mark) or UE2 (on your right just down from UE1 on the Druid Arch Trail). Either site positions you nicely for a side trip that night or the next morning up to awesome Druid Arch.

When heading north down Upper Elephant Canyon, the trail follows the dry wash all the way. In a few places you might not be able to see the trail, but don't fret. It stays right in the canyon bottom until you reach the Chesler Park junction, and you can see strategically located cairns in most cases. Turn right (east) at this junction. From here the trail climbs out of Elephant Canyon. In 0.6 mile you see another junction with the left fork heading off to the Elephant Hill Trailhead. Unless you have arranged to leave a vehicle there (which would trim 2 miles off the hike), go right toward Squaw Flat.

The last 3.5 miles back to Squaw Flat alternate between flat sections w.
defined, sandy trails and small climbs over slickrock outcrops. At the 12.6-mile 1.
you'll see the trail up Big Spring Canyon and Backcountry Campsite BS1 on you
right, and then, near the end of the trail, the junction with the spur trail to the campground.

Miles and Directions

0.1   Junction with Squaw Canyon Trail, turn left.

1.1   Junction with Peekaboo Trail, turn left.

2.6   Junction with Lost Canyon Trail, turn right.

2.7   LC1 Backcountry Campsite.

3.8   LC2 Backcountry Campsite.

5.2   LC3 Backcountry Campsite.

5.4   Sharp right (south) turn onto Lost Canyon Trail.

5.7   SQ2 Backcountry Campsite.

5.9   Junction with Squaw Canyon Trail, turn left.

6.8   Junction with Big Spring Canyon Trail, turn left.

8.9   Junction with Druid Arch Trail, turn right.

9.0   UE1 Backcountry Campsite.

9.7   Junction with Chesler Park Trail, turn right.

10.3   Junction with the trail to Elephant Hill Trailhead, turn right.

12.6   Junction with Big Spring Canyon Trail, turn left.

13.8   Squaw Flat Trailhead.

anyon/Big Spring Canyon

lead.

or overnighter, loop.

Difficulty: Moderate.

Maps: Trails Illustrated Needles and USGS The Loop and Druid Arch.

Trail contact: Canyonlands National Park, 2282 South West Resource Boulevard, Moab, UT 84532; (435) 719-2313; www.nps.gov/cany.

Finding the trailhead: (See map on page 131.) Drive about 2.7 miles west from the Needles Entrance Station and turn left into Squaw Flat Campground. After entering the campground area, the road forks. Both forks go to trailheads with access to the same trails. However, the left-hand fork takes you to the trailhead with the shortest access route to the backcountry. Mostly campers staying in the campground use the right-hand fork and its respective trailhead.

The Hike

This might be the nicest, most accessible loop trail in all of Canyonlands National Park. It's nearly perfect for a moderate day hike to catch the essence of the Needles landscape, and because the NPS designated four backcountry campsites along this loop trail, it can also be an easy overnighter.

Immediately after leaving the trailhead, you hit the junction between Squaw Canyon and Big Spring Canyon Trails. You can take the loop either way; one way is not noticeably more difficult than the other. This description takes the clockwise route because it makes two confusing spots in the trail easier to follow, so turn left (southeast) at this junction.

The next mile goes through fairly flat and open country (i.e., Squaw Flats) with scattered sections of slickrock. The slickrock sections aren't steep, but stay alert and follow small cairns showing the correct route.

When you reach the junction with the Peekaboo Trail, take a right (south) and head up Squaw Canyon. This leg of the loop trail follows Squaw Canyon, which often has a flowing stream in spring. Watch for Backcountry Campsite SQ1 on your right about a mile after the junction. If you've been lucky enough to time your hike while the stream has water in it, you'll probably be treated to a course of spadefoot toad music. Please do not wade in the water.

The canyon narrows in places just before you hit the junction with the Lost Canyon Trail at the 2.8-mile mark. If you cross the wash, SQ2 is down the trail about 100 yards on your right. After this junction get prepared for walking over slickrock. After a short section of well-defined, sandy trail along the streambed, the trail climbs up on the north rim of the canyon and stays on slickrock all the way to the junction with the Big Spring Canyon Trail. This is a very scenic section and a good place to have lunch if you're on a day hike.

At the junction with the Big Spring Canyon Trail, go straight and follow a string of cairns as you climb up a short but steep section to the top of a slickrock pass. Here you get a great view of the surrounding landscape. After soaking in the scenery, climb back down to the bottom of Big Spring Canyon. Even though the NPS has expertly plotted the easiest route over this slickrock pass, this section can be hazardous, especially when wet or with children, so be careful.

After you get down into beautiful Big Spring Canyon, you might see some water flowing, especially in springtime. The canyon is narrow at this end but soon widens and stays that way until you get to the junction with the Chesler Park Trail. Backcountry Campsite BS2 is on your left about 1.5 miles down the canyon. BS1 is right at the junction with the Chesler Park Trail.

At this junction, keep going straight (north) and head toward Squaw Flat Trailhead. Here the trail leaves Big Spring Canyon and heads across Squaw Flat. Just before you get to the trailhead, you'll see a trail going off to the left marked CAMPGROUND B. If you're staying at the B Loop of the campground, take a left, but if you started at the main trailhead, take a right. From this junction, it's only about a half mile to the trailhead. The NPS has nicely routed the trail through some large boulders that in one spot look almost like a tunnel.

Miles and Directions

0.1 Junction with Squaw Canyon Trail, turn left.

1.1 Junction with Peekaboo Trail, turn right.

2.0 SQ1 Backcountry Campsite.

2.8 Junction with Lost Canyon Trail, turn right.

3.7 Junction with Big Spring Canyon Trail, turn right.

5.3 BS2 Backcountry Campsite.

6.3 Junction with Chesler Park Trail, turn right.

6.4 BS1 Backcountry Campsite.

7.5 Squaw Flat Trailhead.

44 Big Spring Canyon/Elephant Canyon

Start: Squaw Flat Trailhead.
Distance: 10.8 miles.
Type of hike: Day hike or overnighter, loop (actually a "lollipop").
Approximate hiking time: 5 to 7 hours.
Difficulty: Strenuous.

Maps: Trails Illustrated Needles and USGS The Loop and Druid Arch.
Trail contact: Canyonlands National Park, 2282 South West Resource Boulevard, Moab, UT 84532; (435) 719–2313; www.nps.gov/cany.

Finding the trailhead: (See map on page 137.) Drive about 2.7 miles west from the Needles Entrance Station and turn left into Squaw Flat Campground. After entering the campground area, the road forks. Both forks go to trailheads with access to the same trails. However, the left-hand fork takes you to the trailhead with the shortest access route to the backcountry. Mostly campers staying in the campground use the right-hand fork and its respective trailhead.

Slickrock section on the trail between Big Spring Canyon and Elephant Canyon.

44 Big Spring Canyon/Elephant Canyon; 45 Elephant Hill to Squaw Flat

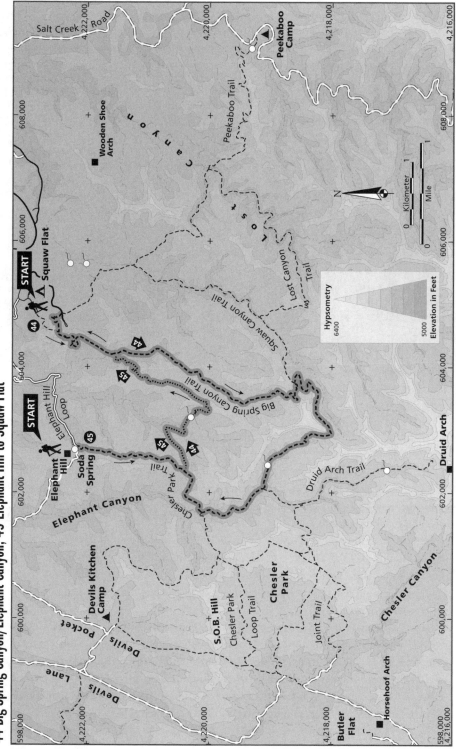

The trail between Big Spring Canyon and Squaw Canyon.

The Hike

If you aren't in good physical condition, this hike might be too much for a day hike. You can make it an overnighter by staying at one of several backcountry campsites along the way. You can follow the loop in either direction, but this description follows the clockwise route.

You immediately hit the Squaw Canyon/Big Spring Canyon junction after leaving the trailhead. Take a right (south) and head toward Big Spring Canyon going through some large boulders just after the junction. Most of the first 1.2-mile section goes through flat, open country with many interesting sandstone features highlighting the horizon.

At 1.2 miles you drop down into Big Spring Canyon, go by Backcountry Campsite BS1 on your left, and then see a junction with the trail up the canyon. If you're following the clockwise route, go straight (south) and head up this gorgeous desert canyon. In springtime the stream is often flowing. The first part of Big Spring Canyon is wide open (watch for Backcountry Campsite BS2 slightly less than a mile after the junction), but the canyon narrows in the upper reaches.

At about the 2.8-mile mark, the trail abruptly leaves the canyon and angles off at about thirty degrees to the left, climbing up a slickrock pass along a string of cairns. Be alert so you don't miss this spot and continue up the canyon instead. From here the trail makes a healthy climb for about a quarter mile to the top of the pass where you get a great vista of the surrounding country. Then the trail drops sharply down to the junction with the Elephant Canyon Spur Trail and Squaw Canyon Trail. You can see the sign from the top of the pass. The climb over the ridge has been plotted out nicely by the NPS but can be hazardous, so use caution.

At this junction, turn right and head southwest on slickrock for most of the 2.1 miles to the Druid Arch Trail. This is an especially scenic section of trail, and in one spot you climb over a pass with the help of a ladder on each side of a joint in the rocks.

Tight spot in the trail between Big Spring Canyon and Elephant Canyon.

A sign marking the end of this section of trail is right in the dry wash of Upper Elephant Canyon. If you're ambitious and in good shape and have enough daylight, you can take a left (south) and head up to Druid Arch for a scenic side trip. However, if you're following the loop trail, take a right (north) where the trail closely follows the dry wash. In a few places you might not be able to see the trail, but it stays right in the canyon bottom until you reach the Chesler Park junction. Turn right (east) at this junction. Shortly thereafter, the trail climbs out of Elephant Canyon. In 0.6 mile you see another junction. The left fork goes to the Elephant Hill Trailhead. Unless you have arranged to leave a vehicle there (which would trim 2 miles off the hike), go right toward Squaw Flat.

The last 3.5 miles back to Squaw Flat alternate between flat sections with well-defined, sandy trails and small climbs over slickrock outcrops. At the 9.6-mile mark, you'll see the trail up Big Spring Canyon that you took earlier in the trip, and shortly after that, Backcountry Campsite BS1 on your right. Then near the end the trail, you'll cross the scenic boulder field you walked through at the start of your hike and return on the spur trail to the campground.

Miles and Directions

0.1 Junction with Squaw Canyon Trail, turn right.

1.2 Junction with Big Spring Canyon Trail, turn left.

2.2 BS2 Backcountry Campsite.

3.8 Junction with Elephant Canyon Spur Trail, turn right.

5.9 Junction with Druid Arch Trail, turn right.

6.1 UE1 Backcountry Campsite.

6.7 Junction with Chesler Park Trail, turn right.

7.3 Junction with trail to Elephant Hill Trailhead, turn right.

9.6 Junction with Big Spring Canyon Trail, turn left.

9.7 BS1 Backcountry Campsite.

10.8 Squaw Flat Trailhead.

45 Elephant Hill to Squaw Flat

Start: Elephant Hill Trailhead or Squaw Flat
Trailhead.
Distance: 5 miles.
Type of hike: Day hike, shuttle.
Difficulty: Moderate.

Maps:
Loop a
Trail c
2282
Moab,
www.n

Finding the trailhead: (See map on page 137.) To fi
miles from the entrance station on the main park road until you see a paved road going off to
the left to Squaw Flat Campground and Elephant Hill. Take this left and 0.3 mile later take a
right onto another paved road. Then take another right 0.5 mile later onto the unpaved, two-
wheel-drive Elephant Hill Access Road. Once on the unpaved road, it's 3 miles to the trailhead.
Drive slowly on this road, especially around several blind corners.

The Hike

If your party has two vehicles, or you're staying at the Squaw Flat Campground and
one member of your party volunteers to drop you off at Elephant Hill Trailhead, this
is a great day hike. Although the Needles District has a great variety of quality hiking opportunities, there aren't many hikes in the moderate, 5-mile range, so if that
suits you, this trail is an excellent choice. You can do the shuttle in reverse, but this
description starts at Elephant Hill Trailhead.

Right after leaving Elephant Hill Trailhead, the trail climbs a steep but short hill
and then goes through a small joint between two rock formations. Then the trail
heads over a fairly flat stretch of slickrock with a good view of Big Spring Canyon
off to the east and the Needles to the south.

At the 1.5-mile mark, you reach a junction with the Chesler Park Trail going to
the right. Go left (east) and head toward Big Spring Canyon. This stretch of trail is
pleasant walking as it alternates between well-defined packed dirt and short slickrock sections. At the 3.8-mile mark, you see the Big Spring Canyon Trail coming in
from the right and Backcountry Campsite BS1 straight ahead. If you want an easy
backpacking trip, you could try to reserve this campsite and spend the night in the
desert before covering the last 1.2 miles back to Squaw Flat Trailhead or Campground. If you're heading for the campground, watch for a cutoff trail going off to
the left just before you reach the trailhead.

Miles and Directions

1.5   Junction with trail to Squaw Flat Trailhead, turn left.

3.8   Junction with Big Spring Canyon Trail, turn left.

4.8   Cutoff trail to Squaw Flat Campground.

5.0   Squaw Flat Trailhead.

ch

Hill Trailhead.
0.8 miles.
ike: Long day hike or overnighter,
nd-back.
ficulty: Moderate.

Maps: Trails Illustrated Needles and USGS The Loop and Druid Arch.
Trail contact: Canyonlands National Park, 2282 South West Resource Boulevard, Moab, UT 84532; (435) 719-2313; www.nps.gov/cany.

Finding the trailhead: (See map on page 144.) To find the Elephant Hill Trailhead, drive 3.1 miles from the entrance station on the main park road until you see a paved road going off to the left to Squaw Flat Campground and Elephant Hill. Take this left and 0.3 mile later take a right onto another paved road. Then take another right 0.5 mile later onto the unpaved, two-wheel-drive Elephant Hill Access Road. Once on the unpaved road, it's 3 miles to the trailhead. Drive slowly on this road, especially around several blind corners.

The Hike

Druid Arch is one of the most popular destinations in the Needles District. In addition to seeing a spectacular arch, however, hikers can experience much of the special environment of the Needles area on the trail to the arch.

You can reach Druid Arch from several routes, but the most commonly used route is the out-and-back route from Elephant Hill Trailhead.

Shortly after leaving the trailhead, you pass through a joint between two rock formations and then go over a stretch of slickrock before reaching the first junction at the 1.5-mile mark. The left fork goes to Squaw Flat Campground. You go right (west) on the trail to Chesler Park.

In the next short (0.6 mile) stretch of trail, you pass over the small divide between Big Spring Canyon and Elephant Canyon. The trail goes through a beautiful narrow where you get a good view both ways of these two canyons. Then the trail drops into the dry wash of Elephant Canyon, where you see the signs for Backcountry Campsite ME1 to the right (north) and Druid Arch to the left (south). Most hikers staying overnight choose UE1 or UE2 for their night out, but ME1 is also a great campsite located on a bench on the west side of the Elephant Canyon dry wash.

From this junction the trail stays right in the Elephant Canyon dry wash. You see the trail to Squaw Canyon going off to the left (east). Keep going straight (south) up the canyon wash. You'll see UE1 and UE2 on your right less than a quarter mile up the trail. Most of the last 2 miles of the trail to Druid Arch stays right in the dry wash of Elephant Canyon, sometimes leaving the canyon briefly on the left flank before dropping back into the dry wash again. Then about a half mile from Druid Arch, the trail starts climbing steeply up to a bench just below the well-named

Along the trail to Druid Arch.

arch, a delightful place to spend an hour or two before retracing your steps to Elephant Hill Trailhead or your backcountry campsite.

Miles and Directions

1.5 Junction with trail to Squaw Flat Campground, turn right.

2.1 Junction with Druid Arch Trail, turn left.

2.2 ME1 Backcountry Campsite.

2.7 UE1 Backcountry Campsite.

2.9 Junction with trail to Squaw Canyon, turn right.

3.1 UE2 Backcountry Campsite.

3.4 Junction with trail to Chesler Park, turn left.

5.4 Druid Arch.

46 Druid Arch; 47 Chesler Park/Devils Kitchen

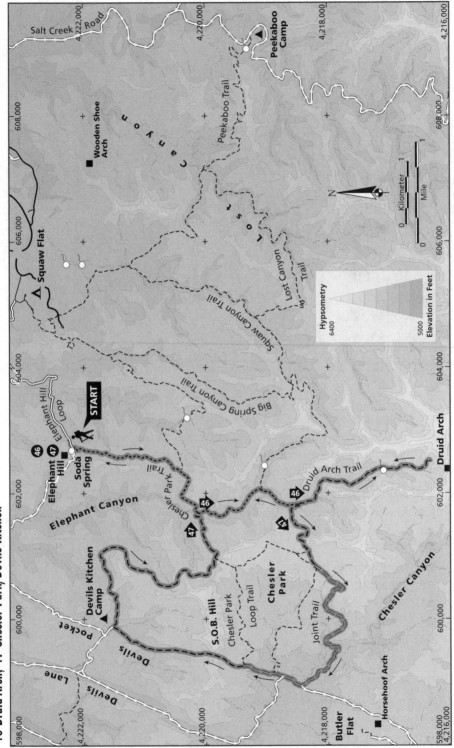

47 Chesler Park/Devils Kitchen

Start: Elephant Hill Trailhead.
Distance: 13.9 miles.
Type of hike: Long day hike or overnighter, loop (actually a "lollipop").
Difficulty: Moderate but long.

Maps: Trails Illustrated Needles and USGS The Loop and Druid Arch.
Trail contact: Canyonlands National Park, 2282 South West Resource Boulevard, Moab, UT 84532; (435) 719-2313; www.nps.gov/cany.

Finding the trailhead: (See map on page 144.) To find the Elephant Hill Trailhead, drive 3.1 miles from the entrance station on the main park road until you see a paved road going off to the left to Squaw Flat Campground and Elephant Hill. Take this left and 0.3 mile later take a right onto another paved road. Then take another right 0.5 mile later onto the unpaved, two-wheel-drive Elephant Hill Access Road. Once on the unpaved road, it's 3 miles to the trailhead. Drive slowly on this road, especially around several blind corners.

The Hike

This is the type of hike that can be crafted out of the Needles Trails Complex. The trip can vary in number of nights out, can be taken clockwise or counterclockwise, and can start and finish at three different trailheads: Elephant Hill, Chesler Park, or Devils Kitchen. This description takes the clockwise route from the Elephant Hill Trailhead, mainly because you can reach this trailhead with any vehicle. You need a high-clearance four-wheel-drive vehicle to get to the Chesler Park or Devils Kitchen Trailheads.

This long loop goes through myriad trail junctions, so keep your map out at all times and keep your bearings, lest you get on the wrong trail. It's fairly easy to get on the wrong trail with all the junctions and trails and canyons that look alike.

This description covers the two-night option, but you can also do this one fairly easy in one night out or extend it to three. Here is a summary of options:

Length of Trip	Backcountry Campsite	Miles Per Day	Side Trip
One night	1—DP1	1—8.4 miles 2—5.5 miles	Chesler Park Overlook
Two nights	1—CP2,3,4, or 5 2—DP1	1—4.5 miles 2—3.9 miles 3—5.5 miles	Druid Arch Chesler Park Overlook
Three nights	1—CP2,3,4 or 5 2—same camp 3—DP1	1—4.5 miles 2—none. 3—3.9 miles 4—5.5 miles	Big Spring Canyon Druid Arch Chesler Park Overlook

NOTE: Be sure to get a map from the NPS showing exact locations of backcountry campsites.

Leaving Elephant Hill Trailhead, the trail starts out ominously, climbing a short but steep hill and then passing through a small joint between two rock formations. Then the trail levels out for a pleasant 0.5 mile walk on slickrock with expansive Big Spring Canyon off to the east and a good view of the Needles to the south.

At the first junction (at the 1.5-mile mark), take a right (west) and continue toward Chesler Park. The left trail goes to Squaw Flat Campground. About a quarter mile down the trail, you climb through a notch in the sandstone spires that is the divide between Big Spring Canyon and Elephant Canyon. Take a few minutes to enjoy the view both ways from the divide. About a quarter mile later, you reach the next junction in the dry wash of Elephant Canyon. Take the sharp left (south) to Druid Arch, which goes right up the dry wash. If you planned extra nights out and had a late start, you could stay at ME1, which is just off to the right about a quarter mile north on a scenic bench on the west rim of the dry wash.

Just past the junction with the trail going to Squaw Canyon, you'll see UE1 off to the right, another possible campsite for hikers who started late or wanted to have time to do the Druid Arch side trip on the first day out. Same goes for UE2, which is 0.2 mile past the junction with the trail going off to the left (east) to Squaw Canyon, another great side trip for hikers staying at UE1 or UE2.

At the 3.4-mile mark, you reach the side trail going up to Chesler Park. If you're camping in Chesler Park (an excellent choice for the second night out) and have plenty of time, you could stash your pack here and spend a couple of hours hiking to Druid Arch.

To reach Chesler Park, take a right (west) at the Druid Arch junction and go 1 mile to the junction with the Joint Trail on the southeast corner of Chesler Park. If you're spending the night at Chesler Park (and you would be fortunate to have the opportunity), about 100 feet down the trail you first see the turn to the right to backcountry campsites CP3, CP4, and CP5. If you have a permit for CP2, it's another 50 feet down the trail on your left. All these campsites could be described as a luxury suite in a five-star hotel. They're nestled in the huge sandstone boulders and spires surrounding Chesler Park, providing shade when needed and a great view out into the park. If you want to extend your trip from two nights to three nights, you might want to stay here two nights and spend the extra day taking short side trips from camp.

When you leave your camp in Chesler Park, head west on the Joint Trail for another 0.7 mile until you see a sign pointing to a side trail going left to the Chesler Park Overlook. Although you've already seen Chesler Park, you get an especially grand view from this official overlook. You would be wise to drop your pack and hike the short trail to the viewpoint.

After you get your pack back on, you immediately drop down into the famed Joint, a seemingly endless section of trail that follows a long crack in the sandstone. In places it gets difficult to fit an overstuffed backpack, but on a hot day, it's a welcome relief from the desert sun.

Hiking to Chesler Park from Elephant Hill Trailhead; the area's namesake, the Needles formation, is in the background.

After about a quarter mile in the Joint, you finally break out into the sunlight again. From here, it's about a half mile on a fairly rocky trail to the Chesler Park Trailhead, where you find a vault toilet and picnic tables. From here, unfortunately, you have to take a short hike on a backcountry road. Walk down the road for 0.5 mile, where you see the road to Beef Basin heading off to the left (south). Go right for another 0.3 mile until you see the Devils Pocket Trail veering off to the right. There is no sign right on the side of the road here. Instead it's about 30 feet down the trail, so be sure not to miss the turn and keep walking down the road.

This trail starts out through a flat, brushy meadow. After 0.8 mile, you see the Chesler Park Loop Trail going off to the right (east). Take a left here and make a fairly serious climb through a pass in the enormous Pinnacle Formation. After the pass the trail drops into another dry, brush-covered flat called Devils Pocket.

Shortly thereafter you see the short side trail to the DP1 Backcountry Campsite going off to the right. The campsite is about a quarter mile from the trail amid some large boulders and piñon pine trees. This is your best choice for your second (or third) night out, leaving a moderate 5.5 miles for the third or fourth and last day of your hike.

After leaving DP1, it's only about a half mile to Devils Kitchen Camp, where you can find a vault toilet and picnic tables and four vehicle campsites. The Devils Pocket Trail ends right at the road in Devils Kitchen and then heads out the east side of the vehicle camp. There are several unofficial trails that have been made by visitors leaving this popular campground, so make sure you're on the right trail. Watch for the cairn-lined trail heading east near the vault toilet on the east end of the campsites. If there's any question in your mind, check the topo map and compass to make sure you don't have to backtrack to find the official trail.

After hiking 2.3 miles from Devils Kitchen, turn left (east) onto the trail to Elephant Hill Trailhead. On this short (0.6-mile) section of trail, you get some fantastic views of the Pinnacle and the Needles before dropping into the dry wash of Elephant Canyon. From here take a short trail north down the canyon to ME1 if you've decided to camp there.

If you're heading back to your vehicle, go across the dry wash on another 0.6-mile section of trail to the junction with the Squaw Flat Trail where you take a left (north) and go the final 1.5 miles back to Elephant Hill Trailhead.

Miles and Directions

1.5 Junction with Squaw Flat Trail, turn right.

2.1 Junction with Druid Arch Trail, turn left.

2.2 ME1 Backcountry Campsite.

2.7 UE1 Backcountry Campsite.

2.9 Junction with trail to Big Spring Canyon, turn left.

3.1 UE2 Backcountry Campsite.

3.4 Junction with side trail to Druid Arch, turn right.

4.4 Junction with Joint Trail, turn left.

4.5 CP2, CP3, CP4, and CP5 Backcountry Campsites.

5.1 Side trail to Chesler Park Overlook and start of the Joint, turn left.

5.9 Chesler Park Trailhead.

6.4 Road to Beef Basin.

6.7 Devils Pocket Trailhead.

7.5 Chesler Park Loop Trail, turn left.

8.4 DP1 Backcountry Campsite.

8.9 Devils Kitchen Camp and Trailhead.

11.2 Junction with trail to Elephant Hill Trailhead, turn left.

11.8 Junction with Druid Arch Trail, turn left.

11.8 UE1 Backcountry Campsite.

12.4 Junction with Squaw Flat Trail, turn left.

13.9 Elephant Hill Trailhead.

48 The Joint Trail

Start: Chesler Park Trailhead.
Distance: 2 miles.
Type of hike: Day hike, out-and-back.
Difficulty: Moderate.
Maps: Trails Illustrated Needles and USGS Druid Arch.

Trail contact: Canyonlands National Park, 2282 South West Resource Boulevard, Moab, UT 84532; (435) 719-2313; www.nps.gov/cany.

Finding the trailhead: (See map on page 150.) From the south park boundary take the four-wheel-drive road 4.7 miles into the park until you see the junction with the road to Chesler Park Trailhead. Turn right here and go 0.5 mile until the road dead-ends at the trailhead. The trailhead has a vault toilet and picnic tables.

The Hike

The Joint Trail is just right for families with a four-wheel-drive vehicle. Getting to the trailhead is the hardest part of this trip.

This is a most unusual hike, an excellent choice for those who want a little adventure (but not danger) and a hike that goes through some very interesting terrain (but not too long or too hard).

The hike starts out uphill on a moderately rugged, rocky trail with cairns showing the way. In about a half mile, it dips into a long, narrow joint between two rock formations. From here it's like hiking in a very narrow slot canyon for about a quarter mile. A few spots require a handhold to scramble over rocks in the Joint, and near the end you climb manmade but rustic "stairs" just before you finally emerge from the depths of the Joint.

Just as you break out into daylight, you see a sign indicating a short viewpoint trail heading right (south) from the junction. The Chesler Park Trail veers off to the left (east). The viewpoint is only about a quarter mile from the sign, but it involves a short climb onto a slickrock ledge. This might be a little nerve-racking for parents, but it's fairly safe. The steepest spots are made easier with little steps chipped out of the solid rock. At the viewpoint you get a fantastic view of Chesler Park—it's the perimeter of stately, multihued sandstone formations including the Pinnacle to the north. After soaking in the view and having a pleasant rest and perhaps lunch, it's back into the "underground" of the Joint again on the way back to the trailhead.

48 The Joint Trail; 49 Druid Arch West; 50 Chesler Park Loop; 51 Devils Pocket Loop

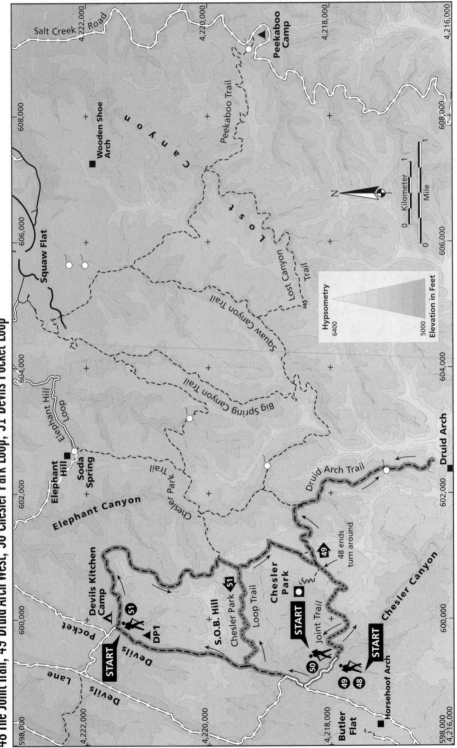

49 Druid Arch West

Start: Chesler Park Trailhead.
Distance: 9 miles.
Type of hike: Day hike or overnighter, out-and-back.
Difficulty: Moderate.

Maps: Trails Illustrated Needles and USGS Druid Arch.
Trail contacts: Canyonlands National Park, 2282 South West Resource Boulevard, Moab, UT 84532; (435) 719-2313; www.nps.gov/cany.

Finding the trailhead: (See map on page 150.) From the south park boundary take the four-wheel-drive road 4.7 miles into the park until you see the junction with the road to Chesler Park Trailhead. Turn right here and go 0.5 mile until the road dead-ends at the trailhead. The trailhead has a vault toilet and picnic tables.

The Hike

The hike starts out uphill on a moderately rugged, rocky trail with cairns showing the way. In about a half mile, it dips into a long, narrow joint between two rock formations. From here it's like hiking in a very narrow slot canyon for about a quarter mile. A few spots require a handhold to scramble over rocks in the joint, and near the end you climb manmade but rustic "stairs" just before you finally emerge from the depths of the joint.

Just as you break out into daylight, you see a sign indicating a short viewpoint trail heading right (south) from the junction.

From the junction of the Chesler Park Overlook side trail, you hike east along the south edge of majestic Chesler Park. The trail is flat, packed dirt and well defined.

Just before you reach the junction with the trail going north to Chesler Park, you'll see Backcountry Campsite CP2 on your right and a short trail to CP3, CP4, and CP5 on your left. If you decided to make this a moderate overnighter, any of these scenic campsites would be your best choice. If you leave early enough, you can set up camp and still have time to hike to Druid Arch. If not (and perhaps even better), get up early the next morning to take the rest of the hike.

Just beyond the campsites, you reach a junction. Go right (east) here and head 1 mile down to the bottom of Upper Elephant Canyon where you'll see the Druid Arch Trail junction in the canyon wash. Take a right (south) to Druid Arch.

The Druid Arch Trail alternates between dry wash and short sections on the east flank of the canyon for about 1.5 miles until it climbs steeply up to a bench below Druid Arch. This is a great place to relax for a while before returning to your campsite or the trailhead.

Miles and Directions

0.5 Start of the Joint.

0.8 Side trail to Chesler Park Overlook and end of the Joint.

1.4 CP2, CP3, CP4, and CP5 Backcountry Campsites.

1.5 Junction with Chesler Park Trail, turn right.

2.5 Junction with Druid Arch Trail, turn right.

4.5 Druid Arch.

50 Chesler Park Loop

Start: Chesler Park Trailhead.
Distance: 5.8 miles.
Type of hike: Day hike or overnighter, loop.
Difficulty: Moderate.
Maps: Trails Illustrated Needles and USGS Druid Arch.

Trail contact: Canyonlands National Park, 2282 South West Resource Boulevard, Moab, UT 84532; (435) 719-2313; www.nps.gov/cany.

Finding the trailhead: (See map on page 150.) From the south park boundary, take the four-wheel-drive road 4.7 miles into the park until you see the junction with the road to Chesler Park Trailhead. Turn right here and go 0.5 mile until the road dead-ends at the trailhead. The trailhead has a vault toilet and picnic tables.

The Hike

If you like to save the best until last, take this trail clockwise. This involves walking on a road for the first 0.8 mile, but it's very easy going, and you're unlikely to see any vehicles.

The road forks 0.5 mile after leaving the trailhead with the left fork going off to Beef Basin. Take a right and walk another 0.3 mile until you see a sign for the Devils Pocket. The sign for this trail is not right along the road, so watch for it a few feet up the trail.

The next section of trail involves a gradual climb up to a junction with the trail through the Pinnacle to Devils Kitchen Camp. You go right (east) at this junction and head for Chesler Park, which is 1.2 miles to the east.

You go through one rocky section with one short, steep pitch before coming out into gorgeous Chesler Park, a huge grassy flatland ringed by colorful sandstone spires. The trail goes along the north edge of the park for less than a half mile before hitting the next junction. At this junction turn right (south) and toward the Joint Trail. Follow the east edge of Chesler Park on a nicely defined and packed dirt trail for 1.3 miles to the next junction. Just less than halfway through this section, you

The view of Chesler Park from the Chesler Park Overlook.

see Backcountry Campsite CP1 on your left. It's back from the trail about 100 yards, out of sight between several large boulders. This is a great choice if you're staying overnight. It's shady and more private than the four campsites 0.7 mile down the trail.

When you reach the junction with the Elephant Canyon Cutoff Trail (which goes off to the east), go straight. In less than 10 yards, you see a side trail to Back-country Campsites CP3, CP4, and CP5 off to your right and, a few steps down the trail, CP2 off to your left. CP2 and CP3 are fairly close to the trail; CP3 has the best view of Chesler Park. CP4 and CP5 are farther away from the main trail and more private. All the campsites are tucked amid gigantic boulders where you can always find shade. You also see some signs of historic ranching operations, which operated in Chesler Park before the national park was created.

From the campsites the trail is flat and easy walking. Long ago parts of this trail were a primitive road. In 0.7 mile you reach the start of the Joint and the side trail going to the left to the Chesler Park Overlook. Even though you've been walking through or on the edge of Chesler Park for a long time, you want to check out this viewpoint. It gives you a grand vista you don't get from the lower elevation trails.

The viewpoint is only about a quarter mile off the main trail and well worth the little climb up to a slickrock platform where you get a better-than-postcard panoramic vista of Chesler Park and the sandstone formations surrounding it.

Back at the viewpoint sign, the trail dives into the Joint, a large crack between rock formations. As you climb down manmade rock stairs to get to its depths, you might think you're not really on a trail, but you are. You stay in the Joint for another 0.25 mile. It's a tight squeeze in spots, but you shouldn't have any problems unless you're built like an NFL offensive lineman. However, you might have to push and twist to get a big backpack through the Joint.

After you come out into sunlight again, it's about a half mile on a fairly rocky trail down to the Chesler Park Trailhead where you started the loop hike.

Miles and Directions

0.5 Beef Basin Road junction.

0.8 Devils Pocket Trailhead.

1.6 Junction with Chesler Park Cutoff Trail, turn right.

2.8 Junction with Chesler Park Trail, turn right.

3.4 CP1 Backcountry Campsite.

4.1 Junction with Joint Trail, turn right.

4.2 CP2, CP3, CP4, and CP5 Backcountry Campsites.

4.8 Start of the Joint and Chesler Park Overlook junction, turn right.

5.3 End of the Joint.

5.8 Chesler Park Trailhead.

51 Devils Pocket Loop

Start: Devils Kitchen Trailhead.
Distance: 5.1 miles.
Type of hike: Day hike or overnighter, loop.
Difficulty: Moderate.
Maps: Trails Illustrated Needles and USGS The Loop and Druid Arch.

Trail contact: Canyonlands National Park, 2282 South West Resource Boulevard, Moab, UT 84532; (435) 719-2313; www.nps.gov/cany.

Finding the trailhead: (See map on page 150.) Driving to Devils Kitchen Camp is only for people with high-clearance four-wheel-drive vehicles and experience using them.

From the Needles entrance station, go 13 miles east on Highway 211 and turn right (south) onto Beef Basin/Elk Mountain Road. The sign at this junction parallels the road, so be careful not to miss it. If you're coming from Moab or Monticello, turn onto Highway 211 and go 20.5 miles to the turnoff. From this junction drive 42.8 miles to the park boundary. This road is passable for high-clearance two-wheel-drive vehicles when dry up to Cathedral Point. Beyond Cathedral Butte the road becomes increasingly more difficult, requiring a four-wheel-drive vehicle, even in dry weather. However, rain or snow can make it impassable. There are a few stretches of clay that get extremely greasy when wet, and this can make the road impassable even for four-wheel-drive vehicles. The rangers at the Needles Visitor Center keep close track of road conditions, so if there has been a recent rain, be sure to check with the NPS before heading up this road.

From the south boundary drive north up Devils Lane Road for 4.7 miles to the junction with the Chesler Park Trailhead road. Continue straight (north) through the junction for another 3.1 miles, going over infamous SOB Hill until you see a junction with Devils Kitchen Road. Turn right (east here) and go another mile to Devils Kitchen Camp, where you find four premier vehicle campsites, a vault toilet, and picnic tables.

You can also reach Devils Kitchen from the north from the Elephant Hill Trailhead. The first 1.5 miles of this road go over Elephant Hill, technical four-wheel-driving most of the way. At the 1.5-mile mark, you see one-way Cyclone Canyon Road joining, but you can't turn right here. Continue straight on this road, which angles south. In 2 miles you come to the Devils Kitchen side road. Turn left (east) and go the last mile to Devils Kitchen Camp and Trailhead.

The Hike

For somebody camped at Devils Kitchen, this is one of two excellent choices for day hikes. The other is Lower Red Lake Canyon, which is longer and out-and-back, unlike this delightful loop trail.

The loop can be taken from either direction, but the clockwise route is described here because it makes the climbs over the two passes through the Pinnacle slightly easier. This is debatable, though. Either way will result in an enjoyable hike.

The trail starts just to the left of the sign at the south end of the campground and heads along a canyon wash for a few hundred yards. It then starts a gradual climb

up toward the Pinnacle, a majestic sandstone formation and highlight of this section of the Canyonlands. The trail alternates between slickrock and well-defined dirt trail for the entire 2.5 miles to the junction with the Chesler Park Trail.

Take a right (southwest) at this junction. You quickly start a fairly serious but short climb to a narrow "pass" in the Pinnacle. At the top of the pass, pause to look both ways for an incredible view of Elephant Canyon (to the northeast) and Chesler Park (to the southwest). It's a very short section of trail, only 0.2 mile to the junction just downhill from the pass on the edge of Chesler Park. If you want to make this an overnighter, you should try to reserve Backcountry Campsite CP1, which is 0.6 mile south of this junction. The overnighter option adds about 1.2 miles to your trip.

From this junction take a right (west) and walk on a packed dirt path along the north perimeter of Chesler Park for about a half mile before heading down a rocky section toward the next junction. Here take another right (north) and start climbing up to the second pass through the Pinnacle.

After descending from the pass, the trail goes through a series of open parks, mostly on packed dirt with a few stretches of loose sand. Less than a half mile from Devils Kitchen, you'll see Backcountry Campsite DP1 on your right. This is an adorable site about 100 yards off the trail and nestled between two big boulders under some piñon pines. The rest of the trail is flat on loose sand until you come back to Devils Kitchen right by the sign where you started.

Miles and Directions

2.3 Junction with trail to Elephant Hill Trailhead, turn right.

2.5 Junction with Chesler Park Trail, turn right.

3.7 Junction with Devils Pocket Trail, turn right.

4.8 DP1 Backcountry Campsite.

5.1 Devils Kitchen Camp and Trailhead.

◀ *A hiker heads toward a narrow pass in the Pinnacle Formation on their way to Chesler Park.*

52 The Big Needles Loop

Start: Squaw Flat Trailhead.
Distance: 22 miles plus side trips.
Type of hike: A multiday backpacking trip (at least three nights out), loop.
Difficulty: Strenuous.

Maps: Trails Illustrated Needles and USGS The Loop and Druid Arch.
Trail contact: Canyonlands National Park, 2282 South West Resource Boulevard, Moab, UT 84532; (435) 719-2313; www.nps.gov/cany.

Finding the trailhead: (See map on page 161.) Drive about 2.7 miles west from Needles Entrance Station and turn left into Squaw Flat Campground. After entering the campground area, the road forks. Both forks go to trailheads with access to the same trails. However, the left-hand fork takes you to the trailhead with the shortest access route to the backcountry. Mostly campers staying in the campground use the right-hand fork and its respective trailhead.

The Hike

The Needles Trails backcountry zone offers many opportunities for long backpacking trips, many of them without the problematic vehicle shuttle. The following description outlines one excellent route, but you can customize your own trip by studying the map.

Although this trail description starts and ends at the Squaw Flat Trailhead, you could start or finish at three other trailheads (Elephant Hill, Devils Kitchen, or Chesler Park) and cover the same territory. However, Squaw Flat is the most accessible trailhead, and you can get there with any vehicle. This loop hike is one of the best because it has many interesting side trips such as Peekaboo Spring, Upper Lost Canyon, Druid Arch, Elephant Canyon, and Chesler Park Overlook.

The loop can be done in either direction with no real advantage or disadvantage, but this description follows the clockwise route. In either case plan on a heavy pack, at least for the first two days, because of the amount of water you need to carry.

Deciding on the length of your trip depends on how much water you can carry, how many miles you can cover in a day, and how much time you have available. This description covers the three-night/four-day option, but here's a quick summary of other options:

Length of Trip	Backcountry Campsite	Miles Per Day	Side Trips
Two nights	1—SQ2 2—DP1	1—5.7 miles 2—8.6 miles 3—7.7 miles	Upper Lost Canyon Chesler Park Overlook
Three nights	1—LC3 2—CP2,3,4, or 5 3—DP1	1—5.2 miles 2—5.3 miles 3—3.8 miles 4—7.7 miles	Upper Lost Canyon Druid Arch Chesler Park Overlook
Four nights	1—LC1 2—LC3 3—CP2,3,4, or 5 4—DP1	1—2.6 miles 2—2.6 miles 3—5.3 miles 4—3.8 miles 5—7.7 miles	Peekaboo Spring Upper Lost Canyon Druid Arch Chesler Park Overlook
Five nights	1—LC1 2—LC3 3—CP2,3,4, or 5 4—DP1 5—ME1	1—2.6 miles 2—2.6 miles 3—5.3 miles 4—3.8 miles 5—3.6 miles 6—4.1 miles	Peekaboo Spring Upper Lost Canyon Druid Arch Chesler Park Overlook Elephant Canyon

NOTE: Be sure to get a map from the NPS showing exact locations of backcountry campsites.

The first 1.1 miles of this hike follow a flat and easy stretch of trail with several slickrock sections. Be alert not to miss the sometimes small cairns marking the correct route over the slickrock. After the first 1.1 miles of easy hiking, you reach the junction with the Peekaboo Trail. Take a left (east) and head toward Lost Canyon and Peekaboo Spring. Most of the next 1.5-mile section is a slickrock. After climbing down a small ladder, the trail follows the north rim of a beautiful, narrow canyon for a short way before dropping into the canyon on a sandy trail for the last 0.5 mile to the junction with the Lost Canyon Trail. Take a right (southwest) here and start hiking up Lost Canyon. In spring a healthy stream often flows through this lush canyon.

When going through Lost Canyon, watch carefully for an abrupt right-hand turn in the trail. There is a sign pointing to SQUAW CANYON TRAIL, but if you're absorbed in the scenery (which could easily happen), you might miss it. On the ground the trail seems to continue into Upper Lost Canyon, but at this point the official trail leaves Lost Canyon and dips into a narrow, unnamed canyon that runs north to south. If you have time you might want to hike into Upper Lost Canyon on a side trip.

When you reach the Druid Arch Trail up Elephant Canyon at the 8.9-mile mark, you find a sign marking the junction right in the dry wash. Take a left and head toward Druid Arch.

After a 0.5-mile walk up Elephant Canyon, you see a junction with the trail going west to Chesler Park. If you're staying out for three or more nights, you probably have time to visit Druid Arch. If so, drop your pack somewhere around this trail junction and take a left for the scenic side trip up to awesome and well-named Druid Arch. When you get back to your pack, take the right fork (west) at this junction and go another mile to your camp at one of the four Chesler Park backcountry campsites. CP3, CP4, and CP5 are on your right just after you reach the junction with the Joint Trail, and CP2 is another 100 feet down the trail on your left. All four sites are nestled in the large boulders surrounding Chesler Park.

After enjoying your second night out on the rim of spectacular Chesler Park, keep heading west on the Joint Trail. In another 0.7 mile, you come to a junction where the Joint Trail drops down into the Joint, and a side trail turns left to the Chesler Park Overlook.

If you want a short side trip, drop your pack here, grab a water bottle and a snack, and take this short trail up to the overlook. The side trail follows cairns for about a quarter mile to the top of a slickrock ledge—a great place to relax for a while and soak in the quiet beauty of the Canyonlands. From here you can see Chesler Park and the ring of sandstone spires that surround it. You've been able to see Chesler Park from your camp and from the trail, but the view is not nearly as dramatic as it is from this viewpoint. After you return to your pack, head into the "joint"—a giant crack between rock formations that goes on and on, sometimes tight enough to make getting a big pack through difficult. Several trails in Canyonlands and Arches have similar joints, but this is by far the longest.

After about a quarter mile in the Joint, you finally break out into the sunlight again. From here it's about a half mile on a fairly rocky trail to the Chesler Park Trailhead, where you'll find a vault toilet and picnic tables. From here walk down the road for 0.5 mile until you see the road to Beef Basin heading off to the left (south). You go right for another 0.3 mile until you see the Devils Pocket Trail veering off to the right.

The Devils Pocket Trail starts out through a flat, brushy meadow. After 0.8 mile, you see the Chesler Park Loop Trail going off to the right (east). Take a left and make a fairly serious climb through a pass in the enormous Pinnacle Formation. After the pass, the trail drops into another dry, brush-covered flat, affectionately referred to as Devils Pocket.

In less than a half mile, you see the short side trail to the DP1 backcountry campsite going off to the right. The campsite is about ¼ mile from the trail amid some large boulders and piñon pine trees. If you're out for three nights, DP1 is probably your best choice for a backcountry campsite. This leaves a tough 7.7 miles for the fourth and last day of your hike, but your pack will be its lightest on the last day as you deplete your water supply. (However, if you would like a short hike for the last day, you can go by DP1 and on to ME1, which would mean 7.4 miles of hiking on the third day but only 4.1 miles on the last day.)

After leaving DP1, it's only about a half mile to Devils Kitchen Camp, where you can find a vault toilet and picnic tables and four vehicle campsites. Some maps might not show it exactly this way, but the Devils Pocket Trail ends right on the road in Devils Kitchen and then heads out the east side of the vehicle camp. The trail out of

The Big Needles Loop

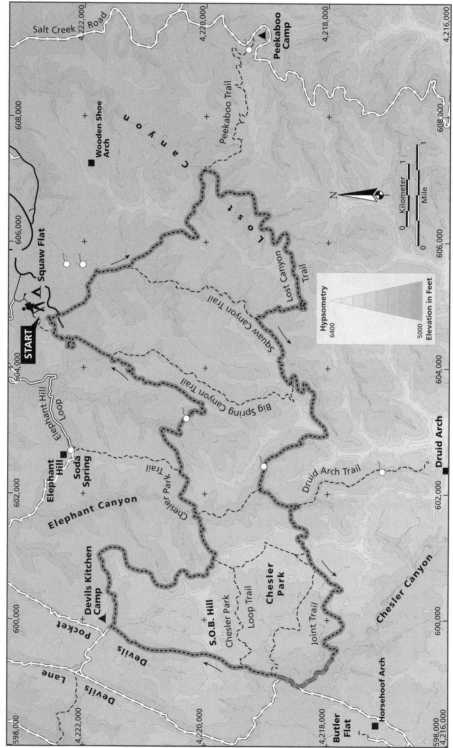

Devils Kitchen is confusing. There are several unofficial trails that have been made by visitors of the popular campground. Watch for the cairn-lined trail heading east from the vault toilet on the east end of the campsites. If there's any question in your mind, check the topo map and compass to make sure you don't have to backtrack to find the official trail.

After hiking 2.3 miles from Devils Kitchen, turn left (east) onto the trail to Elephant Hill Trailhead. On this short (0.6-mile) section of trail, you get fantastic views of the Pinnacle and the Needles before dropping into the dry wash of Elephant Canyon. From here take a short trail north down the canyon to ME1 if you've decided to camp there.

If you're heading back to your vehicle, go across the dry wash on another 0.6-mile section of trail to a junction where you have a choice of trailheads. If your party had two vehicles, you may have left one at Elephant Hill Trailhead and can cut 2.3 miles off your trip. If so, take a left (north) to Elephant Hill. If not, take a right (east) to Squaw Flat Trailhead.

Miles and Directions

0.1 Junction with Squaw Canyon Trail, turn left.

1.1 Junction with Peekaboo Trail, turn left.

2.6 Junction with Lost Canyon Trail, turn right.

2.7 LC1 Backcountry Campsite.

3.8 LC2 Backcountry Campsite.

5.2 LC3 Backcountry Campsite.

5.4 Sharp right turn (south) onto Lost Canyon Trail.

5.7 SQ2 Backcountry Campsite.

5.9 Junction with Squaw Canyon Trail, turn left.

6.8 Junction with Big Spring Canyon Trail, turn left.

8.9 Junction with Druid Arch Trail, turn left.

9.4 Junction with Druid Arch West Trail, turn right.

10.4 Junction with Joint Trail, turn right.

10.5 CP2, CP3, CP4, and CP5 Backcountry Campsites.

11.1 Spur trail to Chesler Park Overlook and start of the Joint, turn left.

11.9 Chesler Park Trailhead.

12.4 Junction with road to Beef Basin, turn right.

12.6 Trailhead for Devils Pocket Trail.

13.4 Junction with Chesler Park Loop Trail, turn left.

14.3 DP1 Backcountry Campsite.

14.8 Devils Kitchen Camp and Trailhead.

17.1 Junction with trail to Elephant Hill Trailhead and Squaw Canyon, turn left.

17.9   Elephant Canyon dry wash, UE1 Backcountry Campsite,
and junction with Druid Arch Trail, turn left.

18.5   Junction with trail to Elephant Hill Trailhead, turn right.

20.8   Junction with Big Spring Canyon Trail, turn left.

21.7   Junction with cutoff trail to Squaw Flat Campground, turn right.

22.0   Squaw Flat Trailhead.

53 Lower Red Lake

Start: Devils Kitchen Trailhead.
Distance: 11.8 miles.
Type of hike: Day hike or overnighter, out-and-back.
Difficulty: Strenuous.

Maps: Trails Illustrated Needles and USGS The Loop and Spanish Bottom.
Trail contact: Canyonlands National Park, 2282 South West Resource Boulevard, Moab, UT 84532; (435) 719–2313; www.nps.gov/cany.

Finding the trailhead: (See map on page 164.) Driving to Devils Kitchen Camp is only for people with high-clearance four-wheel-drive vehicles and experience using them.

From the Needles entrance station, go 13 miles east on Highway 211 and turn right (south) onto Beef Basin/Elk Mountain Road. The sign at this junction parallels the road, so be careful not to miss it. If you're coming from Moab or Monticello, turn onto Highway 211 and go 20.5 miles to the turnoff. From this junction drive 42.8 miles to the park boundary. This road is passable for high-clearance two-wheel-drive vehicles when dry up to Cathedral Point. Beyond Cathedral Butte the road becomes increasingly more difficult, requiring a four-wheel-drive vehicle, even in dry weather. However, rain or snow can make it impassable. There are a few stretches of clay that get extremely greasy when wet, and this can make the road impassable even for four-wheel-drive vehicles. The rangers at the Needles Visitor Center keep close track of road conditions, so if there has been a recent rain, be sure to check with the NPS before heading up this road.

From the south boundary drive north up Devils Lane Road for 4.7 miles to the junction with the Chesler Park Trailhead road. Continue straight (north) through the junction for another 3.1 miles, going over infamous SOB Hill until you see a junction with Devils Kitchen Road. Turn right (east here) and go another mile to Devils Kitchen Camp, where you find four premier vehicle campsites, a vault toilet, and picnic tables.

You can also reach Devils Kitchen from the north from the Elephant Hill Trailhead. The first 1.5 miles of this road go over Elephant Hill, technical four-wheel-driving most of the way. At the 1.5-mile mark, you see one-way Cyclone Canyon Road joining, but you can't turn right here. Continue straight on this road, which angles south. In 2 miles you come to the Devils Kitchen side road. Turn left (east) and go the last mile to Devils Kitchen Camp and Trailhead.

Lower Red Lake

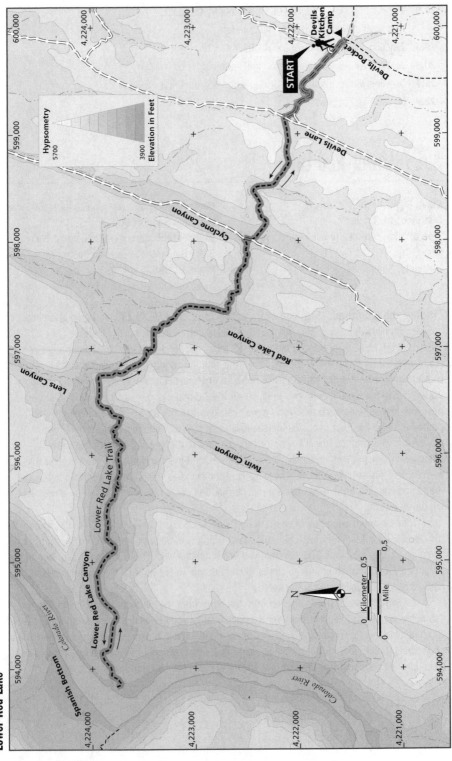

The Hike

This is a long, hot, steep trail, but it goes into one of the most remote and little used sections of Canyonlands National Park. You stand a good chance of having the trail all to yourself.

From Devils Kitchen Camp, you can drive about a mile to the junction with the Devils Lane Road where you see the trailhead for the Lower Red Lake Trail going straight off to the west. However, there is no parking area at the trailhead, so it's best to leave your vehicle in Devils Kitchen Camp and hike from there.

From the trailhead the trail goes over a small ridge for 0.9 mile to the recently abandoned Cyclone Canyon Road. This is easy walking on a well-defined trail. Until 1996, hikers could cut this first mile off the trip by driving around the Cyclone Canyon Road to this point, but the NPS is converting the last stretch of the Cyclone Canyon Road to a trail.

Once across the road the trail starts getting rougher and rougher as it drops into Red Lake Canyon. This is the start of an 800-foot descent to the Colorado River.

Once at the bottom of Red Lake Canyon, the trail angles off to the right and more or less stays in the canyon bottom the rest of the way to the river. Less than a half mile down the trail, it turns left toward the river. A mile or so later, you see impressive Lens Canyon joining from the north. Lower Red Lake Canyon is steep-walled and rugged the rest of the way.

The terrain flattens out somewhat when you reach the river, but regrettably, the area has been burned and invaded by the evil tamarisk, which now dominates the riverbank.

You can camp at-large along Lower Red Lake Canyon, but in this steep canyon it's difficult to find a good campsite. If you're on a long day hike, take a long rest at the river. It's a steep climb back up to Devils Kitchen.

Miles and Directions

1.0 Devils Lane Road.

1.9 Cyclone Canyon Road.

2.7 Lower Red Lake Canyon.

4.0 Lens Canyon.

5.9 Colorado River.

CANYONLANDS NATIONAL PARK:
The Maze, Orange Cliffs, and Horseshoe Canyon

When people use the old adage "in the middle of nowhere," they could easily be talking about the Maze, and it would be a compliment.

Most people have never been to a place as remote as the Maze, and getting there can be a great warm-up for experiencing this remote district on Canyonlands National Park. Whether you come from Hite, Hanksville, or Green River, you definitely get the feeling of being out of touch with civilization long before you reach the park boundary. Once you start slowly maneuvering your vehicle up the primitive roads into the Maze, you complete the feeling of being totally self-reliant. The allure of extreme remoteness experienced in the Maze can't be found in most national parks.

Self-reliance is the undertone of the management policy of the Maze District. This network of twisted sandstone canyons is for rugged individuals who can take care of themselves and their vehicle. There's no gas station, restaurant food, or room service for 50-plus miles in any direction. And even those 50 miles don't tell the true story, because it might take half a day to cover that distance on these roads.

The Chocolate Drops dominate the horizon from the Maze Overlook Camps and Trailhead.

In many national parks, including other sections of Canyonlands, the NPS provides great "customer service." But not in the Maze. The Maze District of Canyonlands National Park combined with the Orange Cliffs Unit of Glen Canyon National Recreation Area (NRA) is larger than many national parks, but once you leave the Hans Flat Ranger Station, there are no services—no guided tours, no facilities, no toilets, not even an entrance station. You are on your own.

In the Maze District you should measure roads and trails in hours instead of miles. A 1-mile trail or a 5-mile stretch of road can take three hours to hike or drive. Under any circumstances, don't be in a hurry.

After a heavy rain the clay coating on some roads in the Maze (particularly the Flint Trail) makes them too slippery to drive. Also, in winter months, ice and snow can make the roads impassable. During winter the Flint Trail is usually closed.

Before you go to the Maze District, make sure you know where you're going, what to bring, and how to prepare. This isn't like going to other national parks. If you show up without the necessary gear to survive on your own, you won't enjoy the Maze District—and probably should not try to. Yet, it happens all the time. People show up in a standard rental car that's not supposed to be driven off paved roads, and they expect to get into the Maze. This is a bad idea!

From Hanksville go north 21 miles on Highway 24 and turn right (east) onto a major unpaved, two-wheel-drive road marked with signs for the Glen Canyon National Recreation Area and Canyonlands National Park. From here it's 46 miles to Hans Flat Ranger Station with right-hand turns at the 11-mile mark and the 24-mile mark, both junctions well signed.

From the Hite Marina on Lake Powell, take Highway 95 north 2 miles and turn right (east) onto an unpaved two-wheel-drive road. From here it's about 59 miles to the Hans Flat Ranger Station with several junctions once you get to the park, all well signed.

From Green River go to the middle of town and watch for Long Street. Turn south onto Long Street and follow it to the edge of town, following the signs to the airport. The road stays paved until it passes under Interstate 70, where it turns into an unpaved two-wheel-drive road. It stays that way for 68 miles to Hans Flat Ranger Station. At the 28-mile mark, take a left at the junction with Dugout Spring Road and, at the 46-mile mark, take another left at the Hanksville junction.

If you want to see Horseshoe Canyon (and you'll be missing something if you don't), watch for a small sign at the 41-mile mark that says HORSESHOE CANYON FOOT TRAIL 2 MILES. If you hit the junction with the road from Hanksville, you've gone about 5 miles too far. If you're coming from Hanksville, take a left at the same junction and go 5 miles north.

Special Regulations

In addition to park regulations listed on page 15, the NPS has a few special rules for the Maze, Orange Cliffs, and Horseshoe Canyon sections of the park.

- No wood fires are allowed, either in the vehicle campsites or while backpacking.
- Vehicle campers can have charcoal fires, but they must use a fire pan and remove the ashes along with other garbage. Pans can be purchased at the Hans Flat Ranger Station.
- Anybody using the vehicle campsites in the Maze District or Orange Cliffs Unit of Glen Canyon NRA must have and use a portable toilet (not an ammo can or plastic bag) and remove human waste along with all other garbage. Portable toilets can be purchased at the Hans Flat Ranger Station.
- Backpackers can bury their human waste, but they must carry out their toilet paper.
- Backpack camping is at-large, but there are limits set for each backcountry zone. You don't need to get your backpacking permit until you get to Hans Flat, but you'd be wise to call in advance for a reservation. Don't make the effort to get there and then find out that you can't go backpacking because your chosen zone is full.
- Backpacking group size limit is five people.

- Vehicle permits have a limit of nine people and three vehicles, with the exception of Flint Seep, where up to sixteen people can camp.
- In Horseshoe Canyon, groups larger than twenty people must be accompanied by a ranger. To arrange for a guided tour, call the Hans Flat Ranger Station at (435) 259–6513.
- Pets are not allowed (even in your vehicle) in Canyonlands National Park, including Horseshoe Canyon.
- Off-trail hiking in the Dollhouse area is prohibited.
- ATVs are not allowed in Canyonlands National Park and Glen Canyon NRA.

What Kind of Vehicle to Bring to the Maze

Unless you wish to hike great distances, you can't fully experience the Maze District without a high-clearance four-wheel-drive vehicle. You can see small parts of the Maze with a high-clearance, two-wheel-drive vehicle, but to see the best parts, you'll have to park it and hike long distances. A high-clearance four-wheel-drive is

GETTING THERE CAN BE HALF THE FUN
I'm not sure what the opinions of locals have to do with anything, but when I was on my way to the Maze, I started thinking that I had to drive lots of miles on backcountry roads and I might run short on gas. So I stopped in Green River to top off the tank. Somewhat foolishly, it seems, I pointed at the map and asked the gas station attendant if I could find a gas station anywhere down there. "Gas station? You'll be lucky if you find a building down there," he responded, rolling his eyes at his coworker. He wasn't joking.

Undaunted, I later asked a waitress for directions to Hans Flat. She gave them to me, but said "There's nothing but desert out there, and if you go out there you should have your will in order."

I was anxious to start hiking early the next morning, so I decided to drive down that night. It was a good two-wheel-drive road all the way, but it was really lonely. For nearly 30 miles, not even a light, not a sign, not another vehicle, nothing. I thought I saw a light once, but it was Venus. Shortly thereafter, a jackrabbit jumped out and almost gave me a heart attack.

Finally I saw a sign showing the way to Horseshoe Canyon, and then 5 miles later, another sign and a junction with the left fork leading to Hans Flat Ranger Station. But there were still no lights or buildings until I reached the ranger station. That's nearly 70 miles of remoteness, quite the culture shock for people used to driving on freeways.

So if you go to the Maze, don't worry about getting caught in a traffic jam or, for that matter, seeing any signs of civilization.

absolutely necessary to negotiate the difficult jeep trails in many sections of the Maze. A long wheelbase is problematic in a few spots, but you can usually get through them by backing up to make a tight corner.

The roads in the Maze can deteriorate rapidly when it rains and become treacherous regardless of what kind of vehicle you have. At the same time, fortunately, they dry out relatively fast. If you get caught in a big rain, it's best to wait a few hours for the roads to dry.

Call in Advance

The staff at the Hans Flat Ranger Station is trained to help you and eager to answer your questions on the phone. That's much better for both you and the NPS, because it's much more difficult to deal with lack of preparation once you're already there. Call in advance at (435) 259–2652. If for some reason you can't get through on the Hans Flat phone system, call the park headquarters at (435) 259–7164. For reservations for vehicle campsites in the Maze, call the park reservation office at (435) 259–4351.

Mountain Biking the Maze

Mountain biking is allowed on all designated roads (but not on trails or off-road) in the Maze District. The Backcountry Roads appendix has detailed descriptions for each road, including conditions for mountain biking. If you opt for a mountain biking adventure in the Maze, carefully plan your trip. The NPS offers the following suggestions:

- Take a first-aid kit.
- Check your bike carefully before leaving and take a bike repair kit.
- Take at least one gallon of water per day per biker.
- Take a lock to secure your bike if you plan to leave it to hike. This is better than riding or pushing your bike off the road to hide it.
- To avoid the intense heat of summer, try the spring and fall. Be prepared for coolish and unsettled weather.
- Wear a helmet and gloves.
- If you want solitude, avoid busy weekends and holidays.

Recommended Mountain Biking Routes

You can take the following mountain biking trips suggested by the NPS or you can, of course, map out your own trip. In any case be sure to stay on official roads. Mountain bikers can stay overnight at designated vehicle campsites, which are described as part of the road descriptions in the Backcountry Roads appendix, but they are required to have a portable toilet, so a support vehicle is necessary.

- **East Rim of Horseshoe Canyon.** Overnight trip; 44 miles round-trip from Hans Flat Ranger Station.

- **Panorama Point and Cleopatra's Chair.** Day or overnight trip; 20 miles round-trip from Hans Flat Ranger Station.

- **Lands End and Big Ridge.** Day or overnight trip; 32 miles round-trip from Hans Flat Ranger Station.

- **Maze Overlook.** Overnight or multinight trip; 40 miles round-trip from the top of Flint Trail or 68 miles round-trip from Hans Flat Ranger Station.

- **Land of Standing Rocks/Dollhouse.** Multinight trip; 50 miles round-trip from the top of Flint Trail or 78 miles round-trip from Hans Flat Ranger Station.

Holy Ghost and Attendants at the Great Gallery in Horseshoe Canyon.

54 The Great Gallery

Start: West Rim Trailhead.
Distance: 6.5 miles.
Type of hike: Day hike (closed to overnight camping), out-and-back.
Difficulty: Moderate.

Maps: Trails Illustrated Maze District/North-east Glen Canyon and USGS Sugarloaf Butte.
Trail contact: Canyonlands National Park, 2282 South West Resource Boulevard, Moab, UT 84532; (435) 719-2313; www.nps.gov/cany.

Finding the trailhead: (See map on page 175.) There are two ways to get to Horseshoe Canyon. You can take the hike down from the west rim (as described here) or you can drive into the canyon from the east. To get to the West Rim Trailhead, go 5 miles north of the junction between the Hanksville and Green River access roads to the Maze and watch for a small sign on the east side of the road that says HORSESHOE CANYON FOOT TRAIL 2 MILES. From here drive 2 miles on a two-wheel-drive road to the trailhead.

The Hike

Although officially a "detached unit" of Canyonlands National Park, the Horseshoe Canyon area could be better described as a little hidden jewel lost in the desert. It's definitely worth the time it takes to get there. If you already plan on a few days in the Maze, you won't be disappointed if you spend half a day of your vacation at Horseshoe Canyon. If you're going to the Maze from Green River, Horseshoe Canyon is a convenient stop.

The Great Gallery is one of four major rock-art sites in Horseshoe Canyon, but the fabulous rock art is only part of the attraction. Horseshoe Canyon would be well worth the stop without it. It's a great day hike in a secluded canyon with majestic cottonwoods shading the sheer sandstone cliffs.

Horseshoe Canyon has one other unusual trait. It's one of the few places in the Canyonlands with a fairly reliable water supply that is devoid of the evil tamarisk. NPS volunteers removed all of the "tammies" a few years back, and now cotton-woods and other native vegetation are reclaiming the canyon.

Rangers lead a hike into the canyon at 9:00 A.M. on Saturdays during the summer, but this is always subject to change. Call the Hans Flat Ranger Station at (435) 259–2652 to verify the schedule. If you have a large group and can't fit into the regular schedule, you may be able to arrange a special ranger-led tour. If you have a group of twenty or more, you are required to have a ranger along.

You don't have to go with the ranger, but it's the best way to get a more complete story and history of Horseshoe Canyon. The ranger stops at each of the four rock-art sites to explain the history and prehistory and also comments on the natural history of the hidden canyon along the way. If you want to get good photographs of the rock-art panels at the Great Gallery, early afternoon light is usually best.

Viewing the Great Gallery.

The hike starts out on and follows an old road from the west rim to the canyon floor. Since it's a road, the grade is not too steep. Nonetheless it drops 750 feet in elevation in about 1.5 miles, which can get the heart rate up on the way back. The road is mostly slickrock at the upper end and turns to loose sand as you approach the canyon floor. This adds to the difficulty of climbing back out. Be sure to bring water.

On the way down you can see the remains of historic ranching operations (fences, pipes, water troughs, etc.). You can also see the austere four-wheel-drive road that drops into the canyon from the east rim. When you reach the canyon floor, the trail turns right and follows the canyon bottom for 1.75 miles to the Great Gallery.

A ranger often stays much of the day at the Great Gallery to answer questions. On the way into the Great Gallery, the first two rock-art panels have interpretive displays. Watch for short side trails, so you don't miss any of them. If you do miss them, you can catch them on the way back.

Rock art is extremely fragile and extremely precious, so don't touch any of the figures or disturb any artifacts found in the canyon. These are irreplaceable treasures. Don't cross over the chain barriers placed around the rock art by the NPS.

The Great Gallery

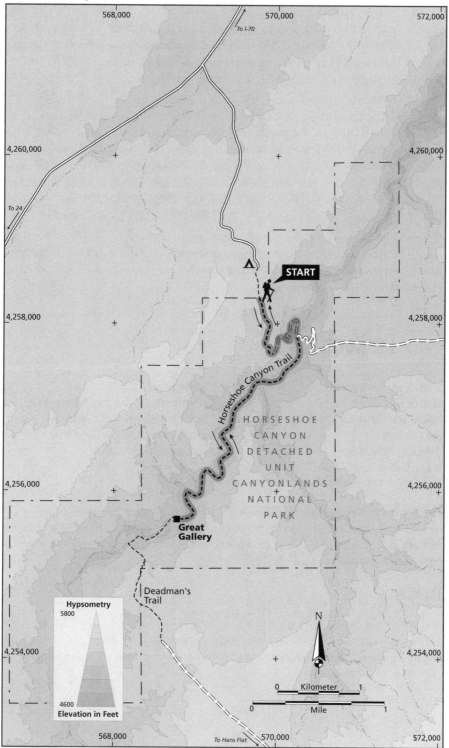

Hypsometry
5800

4600
Elevation in Feet

The rock art in Horseshoe Canyon is considered an example of the "Barrier Canyon" style, which dates back to the late Archaic period from 2,000 to 1,000 B.C. Later the ancestral Puebloan cultures left their marks in the canyon, but apparently stayed only briefly. These early cultures were followed by modern cultures—cattle and sheep ranchers, oil prospectors, miners, and now park visitors. Throughout all this use, however, the special character of the canyon has been wonderfully preserved. All visitors have the responsibility to do their part to keep it that way.

The Great Gallery is the last of four interpretive stops the ranger makes. It's a sprawling rock-art panel with large, intricate figures, both pictographs (painted figures) and petroglyphs (figures etched in the stone with a sharp object). When you reach the Great Gallery, stop for lunch, rest a while, and marvel at a few things. For example, even though the pictographs have faded slightly through the centuries, how did the early cultures come up with a "paint" that lasted 3,000 years? What do the paintings really mean? What type of religious ceremonies might have occurred here? The ranger might toss out a few theories, and the NPS keeps some interpretive information at the Great Gallery, but nobody really knows what went on at the Great Gallery thirty centuries ago.

55 The North Trail

Start: North Trail Trailhead.
Distance: 14 miles.
Type of hike: Long day hike or overnighter, out-and-back.
Difficulty: Strenuous.
Maps: Trails Illustrated Maze District/Northeast Glen Canyon and USGS Gordon Flats and

Elaterite Basin.
Trail contact: Canyonlands National Park, 2282 South West Resource Boulevard, Moab, UT 84532; (435) 719-2313; www.nps.gov/cany.

Finding the trailhead: (See map on page 178.) To get to the North Trail Trailhead, drive 2.5 miles from Hans Flat and turn right (north) at the junction with North Point Road. Go another 0.9 mile and park on the left across from the trailhead sign. You can also park at the Panorama Point junction and hike down the road to the trailhead.

The Hike

For hikers who don't have a four-wheel-drive vehicle or don't want to drive the Maze roads, the North Trail provides access to the Maze. It's for serious backpackers, though, since it's 15 miles one-way to the Maze Overlook—the first 7 miles on

One short section of the North Trail is fairly rugged. ▶

The North Trail

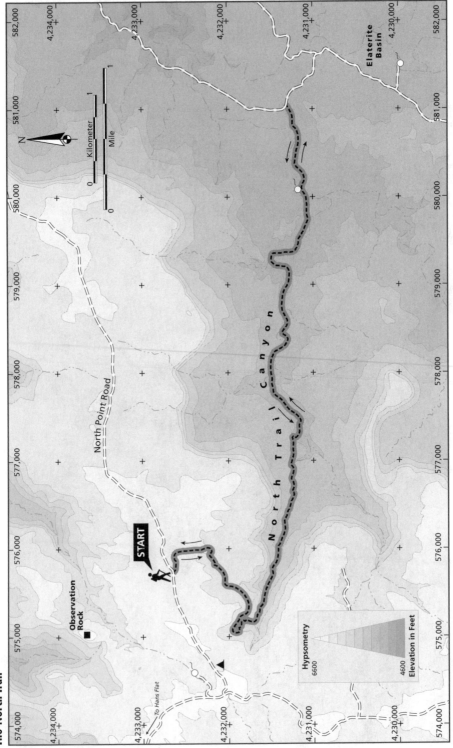

designated trail (the route featured in this hike) and the rest on primitive roads. When you get to the Maze Overlook Trailhead, it's a short but tough mile-long drop into the Maze where you can camp at-large per park regulations.

The North Trail starts out flat and well defined through the junipers and piñon pines on North Point Mesa. After about 1 mile the trail drops into North Trail Canyon. The first part of the descent follows well-marked switchbacks. Then near the bottom there's a half mile stretch of nearly trail-less route finding. There's no chance of getting off the trail, however, since it follows the narrow canyon.

After this one difficult stretch, the trail comes back, but stays rocky and rough as it follows the dry wash of North Trail Canyon for 2 miles. Then the valley opens up, and the trail gets easy and well defined on packed dirt, similar to the first mile up on the North Point Mesa. It stays that way over the last 3 miles to the junction with Millard Canyon Road.

Near the end you cross a small ridge into the West Fork of Big Water Canyon just before the trail-road junction. You're now in Elaterite Basin. Massive Elaterite Butte dominates the horizon to the southeast, and to the north you can see equally massive Ekker Butte and Panorama Point.

If you're continuing on to the Maze Overlook, take a right (south) when you reach the road. If you are returning this way later, note the surroundings. There's no trailhead sign here.

If you plan to stay overnight and then return to the trailhead the next day, or if you started late and need a campsite for your first night on your way to the Maze Overlook, you can find many excellent choices along the easternmost 3 miles of the trail.

56 Happy Canyon

Start: Trailhead at end of Happy Canyon Spur Road.
Distance: 3 miles.
Type of hike: Day hike or short overnighter, out-and-back.
Difficulty: Moderate.

Maps: Trails Illustrated Maze District/Northeast Glen Canyon and USGS Gordon Flats and Clearwater Canyon.
Trail contact: Canyonlands National Park, 2282 South West Resource Boulevard, Moab, UT 84532; (435) 719-2313; www.nps.gov/cany.

Finding the trailhead: (See map on page 181.) From Hans Flat Ranger Station, drive 2.5 miles to the Panorama Point junction and take a right (south) onto Gordon Flats Road. After 12.1 miles, pass by the left turn to the Flint Trail and keep going straight for another 1.3 miles until you see the right-hand turn (west) to Happy Canyon Camp. Turn here and go 0.4 mile to the camp on your left and another 0.1 mile to the end of the road, a parking area, and the trailhead.

The Hike

This trail is actually an abandoned jeep road. That means it has a fairly easy grade, but the lack of maintenance on the road makes the going tougher than it normally would be. The trail doesn't receive much use, so it doesn't get high priority on the maintenance schedule. The plus side of this, of course, is that it's usually devoid of people, so you can have a nice part of the Canyonlands all to yourself.

After 1.5 miles the trail ends as it reaches the floor of Happy Canyon. From here you can strike off in any direction to explore or set up your backpack camp. On the way down the trail, you get a sweeping view of the broad, flat Happy Canyon. You might want to take a few minutes on the way down to spot a few places you might want to explore when you reach the end of the trail.

This is also a great choice for people who have only a two-wheel-drive vehicle. The road to the trailhead can be covered without a four-wheel-drive vehicle, but there are a few rocky sections where you need to go very slowly and use great care. The NPS considers this an "overflow area" and recommends it when the Maze campsites fill up.

Happy Canyon

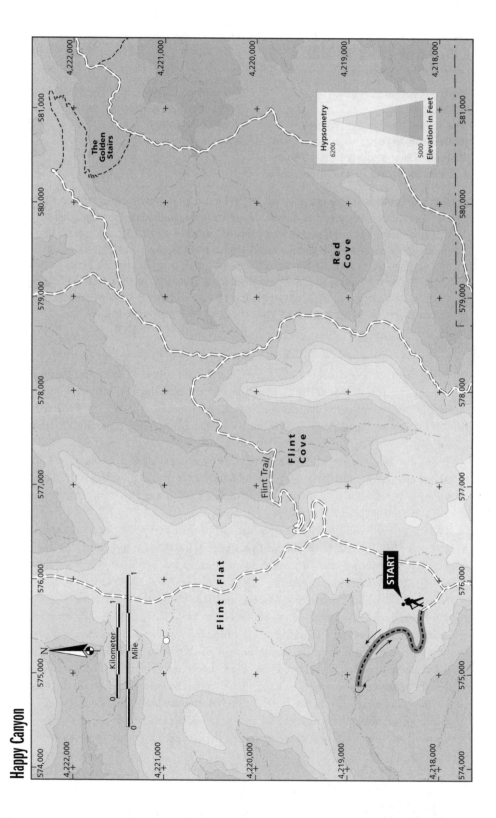

57 The Golden Stairs

Start: Golden Stairs Camp.
Distance: 4 miles.
Type of hike: Day hike, out-and-back.
Difficulty: Moderate.
Maps: Trails Illustrated Maze District/Northeast Glen Canyon and USGS Elaterite Basin.

Trail contact: Canyonlands National Park, 2282 South West Resource Boulevard, Moab, UT 84532; (435) 719-2313; www.nps.gov/cany.

Finding the trailhead: (See map on page 183.) From Hans Flat Ranger Station, drive 2.5 miles to the Panorama Point junction and take a right (south) onto Gordon Flats Road. After 12.1 miles, turn left (east) and head down the Flint Trail switchbacks for 2.8 miles to Maze Overlook Road, where you take a left (north). About 2.6 miles down this road, watch for a sign indicating a right turn (east) to the Golden Stairs Camp. In 2 miles, this spur road dead-ends at the Golden Stairs Camp, a parking area, and the trailhead. The trailhead is on the east side of the camp, not at the parking area where you might expect to find it. The trailhead does not have a sign, so watch for a NO BICYCLES sign and a string of cairns heading off to the east.

The Hike

If you're staying at the Golden Stairs Camp, you'll want to take a delightful evening or early morning walk down the Golden Stairs. For those who don't have the high-clearance four-wheel-drive vehicle necessary to make it over the Teapot Rock section of Dollhouse Road, this trail also can be used as a way to backpack into Ernie's Country.

From the trail you get an expansive view of much of the Maze District, including the sprawling Ernie's Country, the Fins, and even a distant glimpse of the Land of Standing Rocks. You can also see the road to the Dollhouse as it passes through the rugged Teapot Rock Country.

For the first 0.5 mile, the trail passes through juniper and piñon pine on a mesa. Shortly after leaving the trailhead, you pass over China Neck, a narrow "bridge" between two sections of the mesa with steep cliffs on both sides. If you have children with you, watch them carefully.

Soon after crossing the narrow section, the trail drops off the mesa and takes a big curve to the right, gradually descending. The grade is fairly mild as the trail traverses along the face of the cliff until the 1.5-mile mark, where it drops sharply down to the road. During this short steep section, you go through a series of gold-colored sandstone ledges commonly referred to as the Golden Stairs. It's difficult to see them while hiking down, but on the way back, they're much more visible. Also on the way back, you get a great view to the north of the Mother and Child.

Although it's difficult to imagine when you're hiking this trail, it actually follows a historic route once used by ranchers to get their stock up to the mesa to graze.

The Golden Stairs

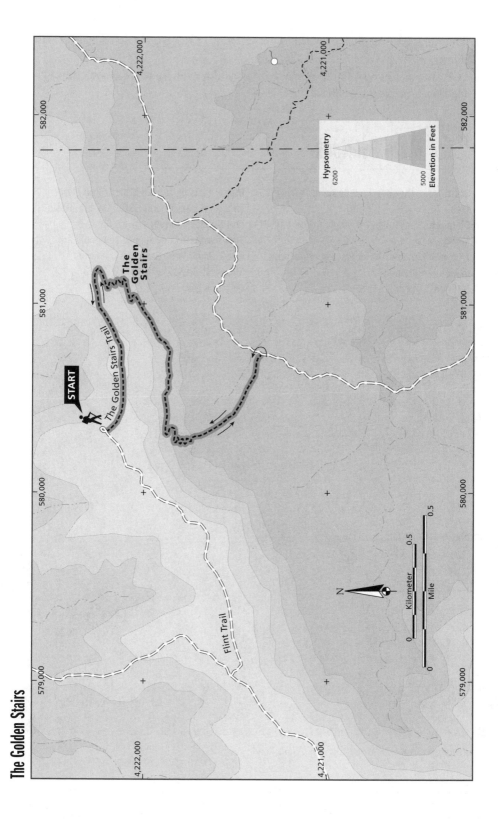

The trail goes over slickrock or loose rock most of the way. It isn't suited for fast hiking, but it's well marked and easy to follow.

At the east end of the trail where it meets the road, there is no sign. Instead a huge cairn marks the trailhead.

58 Maze Overlook

Start: Maze Overlook Trailhead and Parking Area.
Distance: 3 miles not including any off-trail hiking.
Type of hike: Day hike or first leg of multiday trip, out-and-back.
Difficulty: Strenuous.

Maps: Trails Illustrated Maze District/Northeast Glen Canyon and USGS Elaterite Basin and Spanish Bottom.
Trail contact: Canyonlands National Park, 2282 South West Resource Boulevard, Moab, UT 84532; (435) 719-2313; www.nps.gov/cany.

Lining packs down Maze Overlook Trail.

Maze Overlook

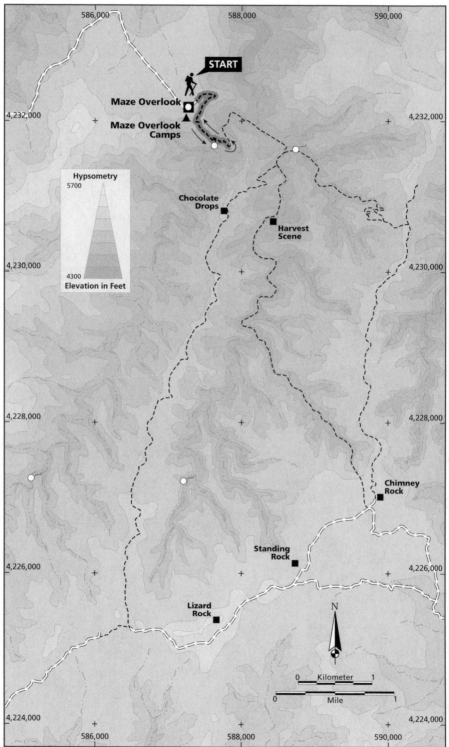

Finding the trailhead: (See map on page 185.) From Hans Flat Ranger Station, take a right (south) onto Gordon Flats Road at the Panorama Point junction at the 2.5-mile mark. At the 12.1-mile mark, turn left (east) and head down the Flint Trail. At the 14.4-mile mark, you hit the junction with Maze Overlook Road. Take a left and go another 8.1 miles to the junction with Millard Canyon Road. Take a right here and go 5 miles to the Maze Overlook.

The Hike

Before you head down the trail, take a few minutes to survey the landscape. They call this place the Maze Overlook because you get a great overview of the well-named Maze. The magnificent Chocolate Drops highlight the southern horizon, and you can see Standing Rock, Chimney Rock, Lizard Rock, and many other famous landmarks of the Maze District from here.

The Maze Overlook Trail is not for beginners or hikers afraid of heights. It's short, only about a mile, but it drops 600 feet in elevation and gets fairly steep and exposed in places, requiring you to use your hands for safety.

Over the first part of the trail, try not to get too absorbed by the scenery and miss the next cairn. The trail meanders back and forth, using ledges as a safe route to the canyon bottom. Then the trail strikes off across the slickrock. It goes through two tight joints, which might be too narrow for an overstuffed backpack. In two or three places, you might want to use a rope to lower your backpack to be safe. Slickrock steps, chipped out of solid rock, help you get down the steepest parts of the trail.

Even though the trail seems rough, it's actually expertly constructed to get down a difficult route to the floor of the Maze. With a little care the Maze Overlook Trail can be perfectly safe.

Once you get to the bottom, you'll see a major seep where, if necessary, you can get water. However, be sure to purify it before drinking. From this point you can head off in several directions, following canyons through the Maze.

◀ *Slickrock "steps" help hikers get down the Maze Overlook Trail.*

59 Harvest Scene

Start: Chimney Rock Trailhead.
Distance: 12 miles.
Type of hike: Long day hike or overnighter, loop.
Difficulty: Strenuous.

Maps: Trails Illustrated Maze District/Northeast Glen Canyon and USGS Spanish Bottom.
Trail contact: Canyonlands National Park, 2282 South West Resource Boulevard, Moab, UT 84532; (435) 719-2313; www.nps.gov/cany.

Finding the trailhead: (See map on page 190.) From Hans Flat Ranger Station, drive 2.5 miles to the Panorama Point junction and take a right (south) onto Gordon Flats Road. After 12.1 miles, turn left (east) and head down the Flint Trail switchbacks for 2.8 miles to Maze Overlook Road, where you take a right (south). Follow this road through Waterhole Flat for 3.5 miles to a four-way junction with Dollhouse Road. Turn left (northeast) and head for the Dollhouse and Land of Standing Rocks. The map might show a cutoff trail where it looks like you can save some time, but this is deceptively incorrect. You actually can make faster time on the longer route because of the excellent roads in this section. Once on Dollhouse Road, stay on it for 17.1 miles to Chimney Rock Camp. At the east end of the camp, you find a parking area and a major trailhead. The trails aren't signed, but watch for strings of cairns heading off on each side of Chimney Rock, which mark the two trails you want for the Harvest Scene loop.

The Hike

This trail is not only a rare loop (most Maze trails are out-and-back), but it's also the longest designated trail in the Maze. If you're in the vicinity with an extra day at your disposal, you will be rewarded by spending that time on this long day hike. You can also backpack and camp at-large in the area, which has several great campsites.

The trail goes to one of the most famous rock-art sites in the world, Harvest Scene. Plus it passes through two beautiful canyons indicative to hiking terrain that has made the Maze so popular. The difference is that you're on designated routes instead of off-trail canyon routes.

Although the routes are designated and marked by cairns, this hike is not for total beginners. It requires some steep climbs and experience in following routes marked only (and sometime sparsely) with cairns. Most of the trail goes over slickrock or follows canyon wash, and there are several side canyons quite capable of confusing the hiker. Cairns mark the trail, but backpackers sometimes set up unofficial cairns to mark the location of their camp and cairns sometimes fall down, so you must be able to find the correct way on your own. Keep your topo map in hand all the way, constantly noting your location.

This trail description follows the counterclockwise route, not because it's easier, but because it's slightly less confusing at one critical spot where you turn out of one canyon into another. To take the counterclockwise route, start on the trail just east

Standing water in an unnamed canyon just before reaching the Harvest Scene.

of Chimney Rock. Be careful not to start on a trail on the far east end of the parking area. This is an off-trail route up Shot and Water Canyons.

The first section of trail stays on top of a slickrock ridge between two unnamed canyons. In some sections the cairns are sparse, so stay alert. To your right you can see into precipitous Jasper Canyon, which is closed to all entry to preserve a unique biological resource.

At the 3.5-mile mark, the trail takes a sharp left and makes a steep but safe descent into the dry wash of an unnamed canyon. This is the most confusing stretch of the hike, so keep the topo map out and note your progress carefully. There are at least three side canyons that could get you lost.

After a mile walk in this canyon, you reach a major junction of canyons. It's not an exaggeration to say that canyons head off in every direction. You need to take the sharp left into an unnamed canyon and head for the Harvest Scene (named on most maps). If there's any doubt in your mind, backtrack or take the extra time to make sure you're headed in the right direction.

Any doubts you have will be erased after about a half mile when you see the spectacular Harvest Scene rock-art panel on your right. (Just before you get to Har-

Harvest Scene

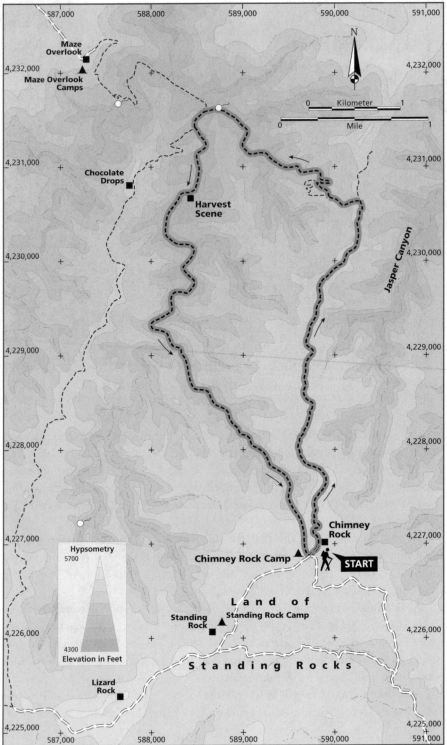

vest Scene, you get a good view of the massive Chocolate Drops formation on the canyon rim near the Maze Overlook Camps.)

Like other rock-art panels, the Harvest Scene is an extremely precious treasure, so don't touch or damage the rock art in any way. It has lasted 3,000 years, and if all park visitors treat it with exceptional care, it might last another 3,000 years.

After a long break at Harvest Scene, continue south down the unnamed Maze canyon, a side canyon to sprawling Horse Canyon. Again, keep the topo map out to make sure you don't accidentally get in the wrong canyon.

Both canyons you follow on this hike have intermittent and unreliable water sources. On many spring hikes, you can see little gemlike pools with their biotic communities of snails, worms, and water striders.

After a pleasant 3-mile walk up Petroglyph Fork, you climb up to the canyon rim. This is a fairly steep but short climb. From this point it's an easy mile or so on slickrock back to Chimney Rock.

60 Colorado/Green River Overlook

Start: Trailhead just before the Dollhouse Camps.
Distance: 9 miles.
Type of hike: Long day hike or overnighter, out-and-back.
Difficulty: Moderate.

Maps: Trails Illustrated Maze District/Northeast Glen Canyon and USGS Spanish Bottom.
Trail contact: Canyonlands National Park, 2282 South West Resource Boulevard, Moab, UT 84532; (435) 719-2313; www.nps.gov/cany.

Finding the trailhead: (See map on page 192.) From Hans Flat Ranger Station, drive 2.5 miles to the Panorama Point junction and take a right (south) onto Gordon Flats Road. After 12.1 miles turn left (east) and head down the Flint Trail switchbacks for 2.8 miles to the Big Water Canyon Road, where you take a right (south). Follow this road along an exposed ledge and down a steep dugway for 3.5 miles to a four-way junction with Dollhouse Road. Turn left (northeast) and head for the Dollhouse and Land of Standing Rocks. The map might show a cutoff trail that looks like it can save some time, but this is deceptively incorrect. You can actually make faster time on the longer route because of the excellent roads in this section. Once on Dollhouse Road, stay on it for 20.8 miles to the Dollhouse Camps. When you get to the Dollhouse area, the road forks with Dollhouse 3 Camp on the right and Dollhouse 1 and Dollhouse 2 Camps on the left. Take a left and the trailhead is on your left about 100 feet before you turn again to Dollhouse 1 Camp.

The Hike

This is the longest and perhaps most spectacular of the three designated hikes in the Dollhouse area. It traverses all types of terrain—canyon wash, open parks, narrow joints, slickrock. It even goes by massive Beehive Arch on its way to lofty overlooks where you can see the mighty Colorado River absorbing the equally mighty Green River and heading south to Cataract Canyon.

60 Colorado/Green River Overlook; 61 Spanish Bottom; 62 The Granary

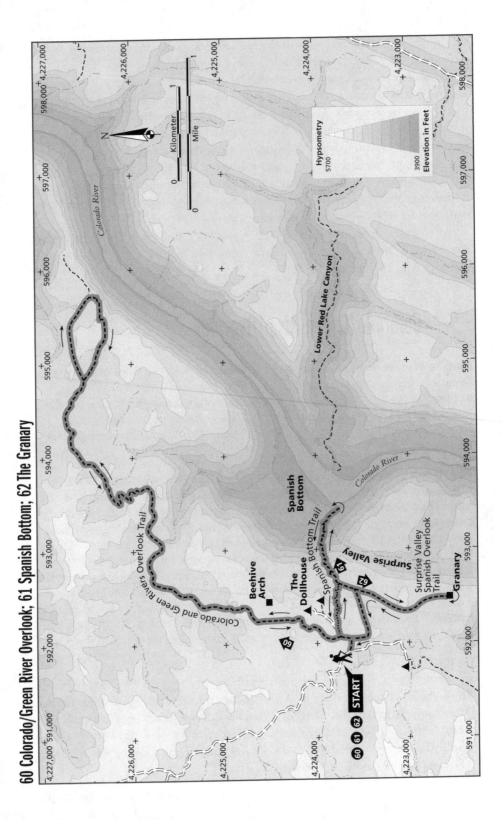

If you have time for only one day hike during your stay in the Dollhouse area, this is a great choice. If you're in the mood to backpack, you can find many excellent at-large campsites along this route.

The first mile or so of the trail wanders its way through the spires of the Dollhouse, going right by Beehive Arch. If you're only interested in a short, flat day hike, you can turn around after investigating the massive arch.

After you leave the Dollhouse area, the trail drops into the dry wash of an unnamed canyon, which forks once with the trail going right. Watch for cairns here; if you aren't paying attention, you could go straight and get off the trail. After about 3 miles you climb out of the dry wash. The trail goes through several open parks with sandstone spires on the horizon.

Next you pass through two narrow canyons between the sandstone formations before reaching the beginning of a small loop. The little loop trail at the end of this hike might not be marked with a sign, and it can be confusing. Get your map out and check it carefully. Along the loop you can strike off to the southeast or northeast along slickrock ledges to get magnificent views of the Colorado and Green Rivers.

On the way back don't miss the spot where the trail leaves the dry wash and goes off to the left. It would be relatively easy to keep going straight and be temporarily lost.

61 Spanish Bottom

Start: Trailhead just before turn to Dollhouse 1 Camp.
Distance: 3 miles.
Type of hike: Day hike or overnighter, out-and-back.
Difficulty: Moderate.

Maps: Trails Illustrated Maze District/Northeast Glen Canyon and USGS Spanish Bottom.
Trail contact: Canyonlands National Park, 2282 South West Resource Boulevard, Moab, UT 84532; (435) 719-2313; www.nps.gov/cany.

Finding the trailhead: (See map on page 192.) When you get to the Dollhouse area, the road forks. The right fork goes to the Dollhouse 3 Camp and the left fork goes to Dollhouse 1 and Dollhouse 2 Camps. Take a left. The trailhead is about 50 feet after the trailhead going to the Confluence Overlook and 50 feet before you turn again to Dollhouse 1 Camp.

The Hike

The Spanish Bottom Trail drops steeply from the trailhead all the way down to the Colorado River, hitting the river just after the Colorado has absorbed the Green River. Even though the trail drops about 1,100 feet in about a mile, it's still the easiest way to get to the Colorado River from the Dollhouse area. The well-constructed trail with frequent switchbacks partly mitigates the steepness. The trail is well defined and marked the entire way.

The first 0.25 mile of the trail is nice and flat as it curves between the stunning sandstone towers of the Dollhouse. Then, shortly after you take a left at the junction with the Granary Trail, the Spanish Bottom Trail starts descending.

For most of the way down, you can see the large and extremely flat Spanish Bottom and the Colorado River flowing by it. You might see some campers, too, since this is a popular campsite for people floating the river. They like to camp here to gather their courage for the thunderous Cataract Canyon just around the bend in the river.

When you get to the bottom, take a break and relax for a while—and, of course, amass your strength for a steep climb up to the Dollhouse. The sharp incline makes this a great trail to hike in the coolish temperatures of the early morning or early evening.

62 The Granary

Start: Trailhead just before turn to Dollhouse 1 Camp.
Distance: 2 miles.
Type of hike: Day hike, partial loop.
Difficulty: Easy.

Maps: Trails Illustrated Maze District/Northeast Glen Canyon and USGS Spanish Bottom.
Trail contact: Canyonlands National Park, 2282 South West Resource Boulevard, Moab, UT 84532; (435) 719-2313; www.nps.gov/cany.

Finding the trailhead: (See map on page 192.) When you get to the Dollhouse area, the road forks. The right fork goes to Dollhouse 3 Camp and the left fork goes to Dollhouse 1 and Dollhouse 2 Camps. Take a left. The trailhead is about 50 feet after the trailhead going to the Confluence Overlook and 50 feet before you turn again to Dollhouse 1 Camp.

The Hike

The first part of the hike (which follows the same route as the Spanish Bottom Trail) is actually part of a small loop. After less than a half mile of flat, easy hiking through the Dollhouse towers, you reach a junction. Take a right (southwest) and head to the Granary instead of dropping off the edge of the plateau to Spanish Bottom.

After another quarter mile of easy walking, you reach yet another junction, with the Granary Trail going to the left. The right fork takes you back to the trailhead, and you take it after you visit the Granary and see Surprise Valley.

Just before you reach the Granary, you see an overlook on your left only a few feet off the trail. From here you get a spectacular vista of Surprise Valley, a classic graben and a gorgeous one at that. About another 100 yards up the trail is the Granary, a typical storage place used by the ancestral Puebloans to hide grain for the lean winter months.

On the way back be sure to take the left fork at the first junction. This follows a well–laid out route through the Dollhouse, including a long stretch through joints in the sandstone formations. The entire trail is well defined, mostly packed dirt and easy to follow.

Checklists

Hiking

Equipment for Day Hiking

- ❏ Day pack or fanny pack
- ❏ Toilet trowel
- ❏ Water bottles
- ❏ Toilet paper
- ❏ First-aid kit
- ❏ Sunscreen and lip lotion
- ❏ Survival kit
- ❏ Sunglasses
- ❏ Compass
- ❏ Binoculars
- ❏ Maps
- ❏ Camera and extra film
- ❏ Pocket knife
- ❏ Flashlight and extra batteries

Additional Equipment for Overnight Trips

- ❏ Tent and waterproof fly
- ❏ Garbage sacks
- ❏ Sleeping bag (20 degrees F or warmer) and stuff sack
- ❏ ziplock bags
- ❏ Paper towels
- ❏ Sleeping pad
- ❏ Nylon cord (50 feet)
- ❏ Cooking pots and pot holder
- ❏ Small towel
- ❏ More water bottles
- ❏ Personal toilet kit
- ❏ Full-size backpack
- ❏ Notebook and pencil
- ❏ Cup, bowl, and eating utensils
- ❏ Lightweight camp stove and adequate fuel

Clothing

In general, strive for natural fibers such as cotton and wool and "earth tones" instead of bright colors. Dig around in the closet for something "dull." Your wilderness partners will appreciate it. Try out the clothing before leaving home to make sure everything fits loosely with no chafing. In particular, make sure your boots are broken in, lest they break you on the first day of the hike.

Clothing for Day Hiking

- ❏ Large-brimmed hat or cap
- ❏ Light-colored, long-sleeve shirt
- ❏ Sturdy hiking boots
- ❏ Lightweight, windproof jacket
- ❏ Light, natural fiber socks
- ❏ Rain gear
- ❏ hiking shorts or long pants
- ❏ Mittens or gloves
- ❏ Lightweight, light-colored

Additional Clothing for Overnight Trips

- ❑ Warm hat (i.e. stocking cap)
- ❑ One pair of socks for each day, plus one extra pair
- ❑ Long underwear
- ❑ Sweater and/or insulated vest
- ❑ Extra shirts
- ❑ Long pants
- ❑ Sandals or lightweight shoes for wearing in camp
- ❑ Underwear

Food

For day hiking, bring high-energy snacks for lunching along the way. For overnight trips, bring enough food, including high-energy snacks, but don't overburden yourself with too much food. Plan meals carefully, bringing just enough food, plus some emergency rations. Freeze-dried foods are the lightest and safest, but expensive and not really necessary. Don't forget hot and cold drinks. Try to minimize food that requires extra water to prepare.

Mountain Biking

Equipment for Day Trips

- ❑ First-aid kit, including aspirin
- ❑ Helmet
- ❑ Duct tape (a small roll)
- ❑ Sunglasses
- ❑ Basic tool kit and spare parts
- ❑ Sunscreen
- ❑ Tire changing tools
- ❑ Pocket knife
- ❑ Extra tubes (two or more depending on length and difficulty of the trip)
- ❑ Head lamp with extra batteries
- ❑ Parachute cord
- ❑ Waterproof matches or lighter (or both)
- ❑ Patch kit (especially if you don't bring two tubes)
- ❑ Toilet paper and trowel
- ❑ Tire pump
- ❑ Notepad and pencil
- ❑ Map
- ❑ Adequate water
- ❑ Compass
- ❑ Emergency food

Additional Equipment for Overnight Trips (without Support Vehicle)

- ❑ Tent
- ❑ Eating utensils
- ❑ Sleeping bag
- ❑ Water filter (recommended by NPS) or purification tablets
- ❑ Ground pad
- ❑ Stove and extra fuel
- ❑ Towel and biodegradable soap
- ❑ Cooking pot and gripper
- ❑ Personal toiletries
- ❑ Cup and eating utensils
- ❑ Cleaning pad
- ❑ Garbage bags
- ❑ Camping permit
- ❑ Book

Clothing

Although quality cycling gear can be expensive, it's usually worth it. For example, well-designed cycling shorts will be worth their weight in gold on the day you wore the low-priced version and started chafing badly. The same goes for jerseys, tights, and jackets. Take a test ride with new clothing before taking a desert trip with it.

Clothing for Day Trips

❏ Padded cycling shorts

❏ Cycling jersey

❏ Long-sleeve shirt

❏ Cycling shoes

❏ Long pants or tights

❏ Cycling gloves

❏ Lightweight rain jacket

❏ Rain pants

Additional Clothing for Overnight Trips

❏ Change of clothes

❏ Warm gloves or mittens

❏ Insulated underwear

❏ Sandals

❏ Stocking cap

❏ Waterproof mittens or overgloves

❏ Waterproof shoe covers

❏ Gore-tex socks

Food

For day trips, bring lots of high-energy snacks. For overnight trips, bring enough food, including high-energy snacks, but don't overburden yourself with too much food. Plan meals carefully, bringing just enough food, plus some emergency rations. Freeze-dried foods are the lightest and safest. Don't forget hot and cold drinks. Try to minimize food that requires extra water to prepare.

Four-Wheeling

❏ Map and compass

❏ Duct tape

❏ Spray lubricant/cleaner

❏ Litter bag

❏ Extra gas in multiple containers

❏ Saw or ax

❏ First-aid kit

❏ Roadside emergency reflectors

❏ Air pump and tire sealant

❏ Cellular phone

❏ Small board to support jack

❏ Sleeping bag and warm clothing

❏ Spare fuses and jumper cables

❏ Extra eyeglasses and sunglasses

❏ Matches

❏ Repair manual for your vehicle

❏ Extra car keys

❏ Water and water filter

❏ Flashlight and extra batteries

❏ Insect repellent

❏ Tow rope

❏ Emergency food

❏ Toilet paper and small shovel

❏ Binoculars

❏ Guidebooks for local area

❏ Camping permit (for overnight trips)

In Addition: Backcountry Roads

Arches National Park

Willow Flats

Start: Willow Flats turnoff on the main park road.

Finding the trailhead: Drive 9 miles into Arches National Park and turn left (west) onto Willow Flats Road across from the Balanced Rock turnout.

Distance: 4 miles from paved road to park boundary.

Approximate time required: 1 to 2 hours.

Maps: Trails Illustrated Arches National Park and USGS Arches National Park.

Permits: No permit required.

Minimum vehicle requirements: Low-clearance four-wheel-drive.

Difficulty: Easy.

Road conditions: Smooth driving on unpaved surfaces, mostly packed dirt, most of the way with a few short rocky sections and possible washouts after rains.

Suitability for mountain biking: Moderate. The road can get seriously washboarded.

Vehicle campsites: None.

Salt Valley

Start: The Salt Valley turnoff on the main park road.

Finding the trailhead: Drive 16 miles into the park and turn left (west) onto the well-marked Salt Valley Road.

Distance: 9.6 miles from the paved road to park boundary.

Approximate time required: 2 to 3 hours.

Maps: Trails Illustrated Arches National Park and USGS Arches National Park.

Permits: No permit required.

Minimum vehicle requirements: Low-clearance two-wheel-drive.

Difficulty: Easy unless road surface is wet, which makes the road impassable.

Road conditions: Smooth driving on unpaved, packed dirt surface.

Suitability for mountain biking: Excellent, although, the road can get seriously wash-boarded.

Special precautions: Avoid this road after it rains. Sections of clay become seriously slippery when wet.

Four-Wheel-Drive Road

Start: Salt Valley turnoff on the main park road.

Finding the trailhead: Drive 16 miles into the park and turn left (west) onto the well-marked Salt Valley Road.

Distance: 16.6 miles for entire loop, not including a 3-mile round-trip to Tower Arch.

Approximate time required: 3 to 5 hours.

Maps: Trails Illustrated Arches National Park and USGS Arches National Park.

HOW TO DRIVE

Of course you know how to drive, right? Driving some of the roads in Arches and Canyonlands National Parks might make you wonder about your ability. The most critical advice given out by the NPS is "don't be in a hurry." If you're on a tight schedule, you probably won't have much fun. You might wreck your vehicle, too, and the towing fee can bankrupt you.

Stay on the designated road and don't widen the road just to miss a mud puddle, small rock, or little ledge. If the road goes over a ledge, that's probably the best route and has been used by thousands of drivers who have gone before you. If each visitor widened the road a few inches, it would soon have a major negative impact on the fragile high desert environment.

Watch ahead for vehicles coming your way, especially in narrow sections or on switchbacks. If you see another vehicle coming, pull over at the first convenient spot. Don't assume the other driver has seen your vehicle or that there will be another good spot to pull off before your vehicles meet.

Permits: No permit required.
Minimum vehicle requirements: High-clearance four-wheel-drive.
Difficulty: Easy to moderate with one difficult stretch between Salt Valley Road and the Tower Arch turnoff.
Road conditions: The road conditions on Salt Valley and Willow Flats Roads are easy, but the connecting road has some difficult stretches. Shortly after turning off the Salt Valley Road, the road goes over a ridge with several tight turns, small ledges, and long rocky sections. Drive this section slowly and carefully.

Suitability for mountain biking: Excellent on Salt Valley Road, but only fair on the four-wheel-drive road and difficult during one long section of loose sand at the 12-mile mark.
Special attractions: Tower Arch and the view of the Marching Men from the junction of the four-wheel-drive road and the spur road to Tower Arch.
Special precautions: It's better to drive this loop in a counterclockwise direction so you can go downhill on one long section of loose sand. In fact, in summer months, you can't drive this road in a clockwise direction.

Miles and Directions

7.1 Left turn at sign marked FOUR-WHEEL-DRIVE ROAD.
9.9 Spur road to Tower Arch.
12.0 Difficult stretch of loose sand.
14.0 Eye of the Whale Arch.
16.1 Willow Flats Road.
16.6 Main park road.

Driving the four-wheel-drive road between Salt Valley and Willow Flats with the Marching Men in the background.

Canyonlands National Park: Island in the Sky

Green River Overlook

Start: Turnoff on Upheaval Dome Road.
Finding the trailhead: From the visitor center, it's 6.4 miles to the turnoff to Upheaval Dome. The Green River Overlook Road turns left (south) 0.4 mile later (same turnoff as Willow Flat Campground).
Distance: 1.3 miles (one-way).
Approximate time required: 15 minutes.
Maps: Trails Illustrated Island in the Sky and USGS Upheaval Dome.
Permits: No permit required.
Minimum vehicle requirements: Low-clearance two-wheel-drive.

Difficulty: Easy.
Road conditions: Excellent conditions on this well-maintained, unpaved road.
Suitability for mountain biking: Excellent.
Vehicle campsites: Road goes by entrance to Willow Flat Campground.
Special attractions: Great vista of White Rim country and, in the background, the Maze District. A skyline locator at the overlook helps you identify the major landmarks. The interpretive display at the overlook explains how John Wesley Powell explored Green River country and found "cathedral-like buttes towering

hundreds or thousands of feet and cliffs that cannot be scaled and canyon walls that shrink the river into insignificance." Today you can float through this section of the Green River and still see the same thing—and be as impressed as Powell was.

Special precautions: Although the overlook is partially fenced, watch children carefully.

Shafer Trail

Start: About a quarter mile south of the Island in the Sky entrance station.

Distance: 6.6 miles (one-way) to the park boundary.

Approximate time required: 30 to 60 minutes.

Maps: Trails Illustrated Island in the Sky and USGS Musselman Arch.

Permits: Vehicle camping or backcountry permit required. Day use allowed without permit. People driving up the Shafer Trail from Moab must stop at the park entrance station and pay the park entrance/exit fee.

Minimum vehicle requirements: High-clearance two-wheel-drive in dry conditions. Otherwise high-clearance four-wheel-drive. Carry chains in winter.

Difficulty: Moderate.

Road conditions: Fairly easy driving with the exception of a few short rocky spots in the last 2 miles.

Suitability for mountain biking: Excellent, but be careful going down switchbacks. Steep grade coming back up to entrance station.

Vehicle campsites: Shafer Camp (one campsite).

Special precautions: Be alert driving or mountain biking down the steep switchbacks in the first mile. Watch ahead and pull over if you see another vehicle coming up the switchbacks. Road conditions change if it rains or snows. When wet you need a four-wheel-drive vehicle with chains.

Miles and Directions

4.5 Bottom of switchbacks.

5.1 Left turn to Moab and Potash, vault toilet.

6.1 Shafer Camp.

6.6 Park boundary.

The White Rim

Start: About a quarter mile south of the Island in the Sky entrance station.

Distance: 72.2 miles within the park, plus another 24.6 miles to get back to your starting point.

Approximate time required: 15 to 20 hours.

Maps: Trails Illustrated Island in the Sky and USGS Musselman Arch, Monument Basin, Turks Head, Horsethief Canyon, and Upheaval Dome.

Permits: Vehicle camping and backcountry permit required. Day use allowed without permit.

Minimum vehicle requirements: High-clearance four-wheel-drive.

Mountain biking White Rim Road near Airport Butte.

Difficulty: Moderate.

Road conditions: When dry it's fairly easy four-wheeling most of the way, primarily on a packed dirt road surface with intermittent rocky sections. The section of road around Musselman Arch gets very rocky, and the sections over Murphy Hogback and between Potato Bottom and Hardscrabble Camps are steep and hazardous when wet.

Suitability for mountain biking: Excellent conditions most of the way, with the exception of numerous but short rocky sections. Steep upgrades going up to Fort Bottom, Murphy Hogback, Shafer Trail, and near the end of the trip at Mineral Bottom. Remember that bicycles stay on the roads just as motorized vehicles do.

Vehicle campsites: All campsites along White Rim Road have NPS-maintained vault toilets. Reservations are highly recommended as sites may be booked up to one year in advance. The campsites include the following:

Airport—Four campsites. Fairly exposed. Conveniently located for first night out on a multiday mountain biking trip. In the shadow of Airport Tower. About 100 yards west of road.

Gooseberry—Two campsites. Exposed. About 100 yards west of road.

White Crack—One campsite. Exposed. Private (about 1.4 miles from White Rim Road). Great view into Colorado River Basin.

Murphy—Three campsites. Right along road. Great view into Green River Basin.

Candlestick—One campsite. Exposed. Great view of Candlestick Tower.

Potato Bottom—Three campsites. Right along road. Short level walk to Green River.

Hardscrabble—Two campsites. Private. Short walk to the Green River.

Labyrinth—Two campsites. At junction with Taylor Canyon road. Exposed. Short walk to Green River.

Taylor—One campsite. Private. Great view of Moses and Zeus and Trail Canyon.

Special attractions: The White Rim Road is, for most people, a multiday adventure. It has incredible scenery and world-famous mountain biking. The most popular way to see the White Rim Road is on a mountain bike, usually supported by a four-wheel-drive vehicle. Most people spend at least three days here to enjoy camping and hiking and to take spur roads into Lathrop and Taylor Canyons.

Special precautions: Unlike many park roads, the White Rim Road gets extensive use during peak seasons. The NPS limits the amount of overnight use with the permit system, but currently day use is not limited. Watch carefully for other vehicles (especially on the steep sections on the Shafer Trail, on the Murphy Hogback, and Hardscrabble Hill near Fort Bottom) and for mountain bikers and hikers on the road. When wet, road conditions can dramatically worsen (especially around Fort Bottom). If you get caught in a rain, it might pay to wait 4 to 5 hours to let the road dry out. Also, be cautious around unfenced overlooks at the Gooseneck Overlook, Musselman Arch, and Colorado River Overlook. The NPS recommends that you carry chains and a shovel as well. Be sure to take adequate water supplies. Store water in multiple containers—just in case one springs a leak.

Miles and Directions

4.5   Bottom of switchbacks.

5.1   Turnoff to Moab and Potash.

6.4   Gooseneck Trailhead.

8.2   Colorado River Overlook.

8.4   Musselman Arch.

16.2   Lathrop Trail.

16.3   Turnoff to Lathrop Canyon.

17.3   Airport Tower Camp.

27.2   Gooseberry Trail.

27.7   Gooseberry Camp.

35.7   Turnoff to White Crack Camp (1.4 miles off White Rim Road).

42.1   Murphy Wash Trail.

43.3   Murphy Camp.

43.4   Murphy Hogback Trail.

53.5 Candlestick Camp.

55.7 Wilhite Trail.

63.5 Potato Bottom Camp (A).

64.7 Potato Bottom Camp (B and C).

66.1 Fort Bottom Trail.

67.8 Turnoff to Hardscrabble Camp (A and B).

69.1 Upheaval Canyon Trail.

69.7 Turnoff to Taylor Canyon (5 miles to Taylor Canyon Camp).

69.8 Labyrinth Camp.

72.2 Park boundary.

76.0 Junction with Mineral Bottom Trail and spur road to Mineral Bottom Launch.

77.5 Top of switchbacks and parking area.

90.4 Highway 313 and parking area.

96.8 Island in the Sky entrance station.

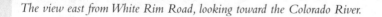

The view east from White Rim Road, looking toward the Colorado River.

Lathrop Canyon

Start: Junction of White Rim Road and Lathrop Canyon, 16.3 miles from the Island in the Sky entrance station.

Distance: 4 miles (one-way) from White Rim Road to Colorado River.

Approximate time required: 30 to 60 minutes.

Maps: Trails Illustrated Island in the Sky and USGS Musselman Arch and Monument Basin.

Permits: At-large backpacking permit required. (This must be obtained at the visitor center.) Day use allowed without a permit.

Minimum vehicle requirements: High-clearance four-wheel-drive.

Difficulty: Difficult.

Road conditions: Extremely steep at the head of the canyon near White Rim Road. Few short slickrock sections. Sandy conditions near the bottom.

Suitability for mountain biking: Mostly good with a few short stretches of loose sand.

Vehicle campsites: None. Day use only. During high water, this area can be inaccessible.

Special attractions: At the end of the road, where it runs into the Colorado River, you'll find a great place for a picnic or lunch break, with picnic tables, a vault toilet, and the shade of sprawling cottonwood, tamarisk and willow trees.

Special precautions: The potential for flash floods is extremely high when it's raining. Road conditions can change rapidly. You might be tempted to jump in the river, but this is not a swimming pool. It's a big, powerful river.

A panoramic view of the Canyonlands.

Taylor Canyon

Start: Junction between White Rim Road and Taylor Canyon Road, 2.5 miles from the north boundary of the park.

Distance: 5 miles (one-way).

Approximate time required: 30 to 60 minutes

Maps: Trails Illustrated Island in the Sky and USGS Upheaval Dome.

Permits: Vehicle camping or backpacking permit required. Obtain at the visitor center. Day use allowed without a permit.

Minimum vehicle requirements: High-clearance four-wheel-drive.

Difficulty: Moderate.

Road conditions: Excellent conditions with a few rocky sections. Road conditions can change rapidly when wet. Flash flooding potential. Deep sand exists when conditions are very dry.

Suitability for mountain biking: Excellent conditions usually. Road conditions can change rapidly when wet. Flash flooding potential. Deep sand exists when conditions are very dry.

Vehicle campsites: Taylor Camp (one campsite) at the end of the road in the shadow of the magnificent Moses formation.

Special attractions: The famous Moses and Zeus spires make Taylor Canyon particularly popular with rock climbers.

Special precautions: Don't try climbing the spires in the area without the proper training, equipment, and experience.

Canyonlands National Park: The Needles

Salt Creek

Start: Salt Creek Trailhead at locked gate.

Finding the trailhead: Drive 0.9 mile west from the entrance station and take a left (south) onto a well-signed paved road (marked SALT CREEK) and go 0.5 mile before taking a left (east) onto a two-wheel-drive unpaved road. About 0.5 mile up the unpaved road, turn right (south) instead of going straight to the Cave Spring Trailhead. Then, go 0.5 mile more until you see a locked gate across the road. This gate marks the official trailhead for Salt Creek and Horse Canyon Roads.

Distance: From the locked gate, it's 3.3 miles (one-way) to Peekaboo Camp and the end of the road.

Maps: Trails Illustrated Needles and USGS The Loop, South Six-shooter Peak and Druid Arch.

Permits: The first step on your trip to Salt Creek is a stop at the Needles Visitor Center to get a permit. You need a permit for overnight or day use. Salt Creek has only two vehicle campsites (both at Peekaboo Camp), so overnight permits are often difficult to get. To improve your chances, use the park's reservation system. You can reserve a day-use permit in advance just like you do overnight permits. If you feel lucky, you can take a chance and simply go to the visitor center and hope all permits aren't taken for that day. If you want to get a day-use permit when you get to the Needles, try to get to the visitor center early in the day. When you get your permit, a ranger gives you the combination (changed daily) to the locked gate at the trailhead. Listen carefully on how to use the combination lock. It can be tricky.

Minimum vehicle requirements: High-clearance four-wheel-drive.

Difficulty: Moderate.

Road conditions: The first 2.5 miles are the most difficult part of the road because you pass through several sections of very loose sand where you must keep your speed up. The rest of the road is easy going with the exception of frequent stream crossings. In spring, some of the water stretches can go on for 100 yards or more.

Suitability for mountain biking: The NPS does not recommend mountain biking in Salt Creek. Loose sand in the first 2.5 miles and frequent stream crossings all along the road would make mountain biking marginal at best.

Vehicle camps: Peekaboo Camp (two camp-sites) is on your right about a mile after the junction with Horse Canyon Road. It's a lovely site under some huge cottonwood trees but quite close to the road, making privacy during midday difficult.

Special attractions: Besides being a gorgeous high desert canyon, Salt Creek attracted many early residents, mainly because of the reliable water sources it offered. As a result, the canyon has numerous ruins and rock-art panels.

Special precautions: Salt Creek is subject to flash floods. To be safe, take sleeping bags; water filter, water purification tablets, or extra water; and emergency food for two or three days. And, of course, keep your eye on the weather conditions.

Miles and Directions

2.3 Junction with Horse Canyon Road.

3.3 Peekaboo Camp.

Salt Creek Road crosses Salt Creek many times on the way to Angel Arch.

BE OBSERVANT A wealth of rock-art panels lies hidden in the overhanging cliffs and high alcoves of Salt Creek and Horse Canyon. Mainly because of the reliable water sources, Archaic and ancestral Puebloan Indians inhabited this area over a span of at least two hundred years. These early residents used the area extensively for farming, which explains the large number of granaries found in the canyon.

The National Park Service has designated the area the Salt Creek Archeological District. In 1975, the district was placed on the National Register of Historic Places. Be extremely careful not to disturb any ruins, granaries, or rock art. If you observe anybody else disturbing these fragile resources, please report it to a ranger.

Horse Canyon

Start: Salt Creek Trailhead at the locked gate.
Finding the trailhead: Refer to Road i, Salt Creek.
Distance: From the locked gate, it's 8.7 miles (one way) to the end of the road, plus the 0.5-mile (one way) road to the Tower Ruin Viewpoint.
Approximate time required: 2 to 3 hours, not including 1-mile (round-trip) to Tower Ruin Viewpoint or any hiking. If you want to drive to the end of the road, take the spur road to Tower Ruin, stop and see Paul Bunyan's Potty, and take the short hikes to Castle and Fortress arches, set aside an extra half-day.
Maps: Trails Illustrated Needles and USGS The Loop, North Six-shooter Peak, and South Six-shooter Peak.
Permits: Overnight and day-use permits required. Check at the Needles Visitor Center.
Minimum vehicle requirements: High-clearance four-wheel-drive.
Difficulty: Moderate.
Road conditions: Although Horse Canyon is, for the most part, easy four-wheeling, you must go through the first 2.5 miles of Salt Creek to get there. This section has several sections of loose sand where you must keep your speed up. Just before the Castle Arch Trailhead, there's one tight spot between a boulder and a cliff where you could leave some paint on a rock if you aren't careful.
Suitability for mountain biking: The NPS does not recommend mountain biking in Horse Canyon. Some parts of Horse Canyon would be fair mountain biking, but several stretches of loose sand would be difficult. Getting through the first 2.5 miles of Salt Creek would make the area marginal at best for mountain biking.
Vehicle campsites: No vehicle campsites, but the parking area for Paul Bunyan's Potty has a vault toilet.
Special attractions: Paul Bunyan's Potty is an unusual (but well-named) pothole arch. Also, be sure to take the spur road to see Tower Ruin, among the most spectacular anywhere. It's in an alcove high above the valley floor. Don't climb up to this fragile site. Instead, just look and marvel about what it must have been like to build it, get water up there, or even live there.

Miles and Directions

2.5 Junction with Salt Creek Road.
3.5 Paul Bunyan's Potty.
4.5 Tower Ruin Road.
8.5 Castle Arch Trailhead.
8.7 Fortress Arch Trailhead and end of Horse Canyon Road.

Colorado Overlook

Start: Needles Visitor Center.
Finding the trailhead: The visitor center is on your right (north) 0.9 mile past the entrance station.
Distance: From the visitor center, it's 7 miles (one-way) to the overlook parking area.
Approximate time required: 2 to 3 hours.
Maps: Trails Illustrated Needles and USGS The Loop.
Permits: No permit required.

At the end of Colorado Overlook Road with the Colorado River in the background.

Minimum vehicle requirements: High-clearance four-wheel-drive.
Difficulty: Moderate.
Road conditions: First 3 miles are on packed dirt and easily passable with a two-wheel-drive vehicle. Then the road gets rocky as it goes over several slickrock sections. The last mile is the toughest—it's mostly slickrock with several significant ledges.

Suitability for mountain biking: Excellent mountain biking.
Vehicle campsites: No vehicle campsites.
Special attractions: Note the incredible canyon gouged out by Salt Creek on its way to the Colorado River.
Special precautions: This is an unfenced overlook with very steep cliffs, so be careful not to get too close to the edge. Keep the kids by your side.

Lavender Canyon

Start: Locked gate at park boundary.
Finding the trailhead: From the Needles entrance station, drive 7.6 miles east on Highway 211 and turn right (south) at a road marked "Davis Canyon." If you're coming from the other direction, this turn is 25.9 miles from

U.S. Highway 191. After turning off Highway 211, drive 13.9 miles on an unpaved road to the park boundary. The first 3 miles have a few rocky spots. Then, at the 3-mile mark, you see a road going off to the right up a dry wash. It's tempting to take that road, but it doesn't go to

Driving Lavender Canyon with Cleft Arch on the horizon.

Lavender Canyon. Go across the dry wash, staying on the road you're driving. There should be a sign indicating Lavender Canyon to the left. A mile or so after the sign, you drop down into Lavender Canyon, and the road turns (south) and heads up the dry wash and stays there all the way to the park boundary.

Distance: From Highway 211, it's 13.9 miles (one-way) to the park boundary. From the park boundary, it's 4.1 miles (one-way) to the end of the main road or 3 miles (one-way) to the end of the west fork road of the West Fork of Lavender Canyon.

Approximate time required: 7 to 9 hours to see both canyons, not including any hiking.

Maps: Trails Illustrated Needles and USGS South Six-shooter Peak and Hans Point.

Permits: Day-use permit required, available at the Needles Visitor Center. At the park boundary, you'll find a locked gate that opens with

the combination the ranger writes on your permit. The combination changes every day, so you must come in and out on the days designated on the permit.

Minimum vehicle requirements: High-clearance four-wheel-drive.

Difficulty: Moderate.

Road conditions: The condition on the unpaved road to the park boundary is good. Inside the park, the roads are mostly packed dirt with frequent sections of loose sand and a few short rocky sections. The road up the West Fork of Lavender Canyon (not shown on some maps) is more narrow and difficult than the main road. Some maps show the main road splitting again near the end of the road, but the right-hand road only goes about 100 yards from the main road.

Suitability for mountain biking: Difficult mountain biking (both inside and outside the park) because of the abundance of loose sand.

Vehicle campsites: No vehicle camping allowed in Lavender Canyon. At-large backpacking with a permit is allowed, but you must leave your vehicle at the park boundary.

Special attractions: Under the right light conditions, the canyon walls such as those to the east dropping down from Bridger Jack Mesa really do get a beautiful lavender color. In the first 0.5 mile after entering the park, watch for two beautiful but easy-to-miss arches on the western rim of the canyon. The first is Natural Arch. About 200 yards later, you can see the second, Caterpillar Arch. Most maps note only one or the other of these two arches, but not both. Cleft Arch at the end of the main road is also an awesome sight.

Special precautions: The road to the park boundary goes through ranching operations on private land and through leased BLM land, so watch carefully for cattle (especially in spring when calves are running around carefree) and respect private property in the area. Be sure to close all gates behind you.

Miles and Directions

0.1 First gate.

0.7 Left turn at an unsigned junction.

0.8 Wooden gate.

3.0 Right turn at a signed junction.

13.9 Locked gate at park boundary.

14.4 Split in road.

17.4 Cleft Arch.

18.0 End of main road.

Devils Lane/Confluence Overlook

Start: Park boundary.

Finding the trailhead: From Highway 211, drive 42.8 miles to the park boundary, staying on the main Elk Mountain/Beef Basin Road all the way.

Distance: From Highway 211, it's 42.8 miles (one-way) to the park boundary. From the park boundary, it's 12.3 miles (one-way) from park boundary to the Confluence Overlook Trailhead.

Approximate time required: 2 to 3 hours (one-way) from Highway 211 to the park boundary (on dry roads), plus 5 to 6 hours (one-way) to the Confluence Overlook Trailhead.

Maps: Trails Illustrated Needles and USGS Cross Canyon, Spanish Bottom, Druid Arch, and The Loop.

Permits: No permit necessary for day use, but overnight vehicle camping or at-large backpacking permits required.

Minimum vehicle requirements: High-clearance four-wheel-drive.

Difficulty: Difficult.

Road conditions: With the exception of three technically difficult sections (South Boundary Hill, SOB Hill, and Silver Stairs), the road is easy four-wheeling, mostly packed dirt with a few short rocky sections and some loose sand.

Suitability for mountain biking: Moderate mountain biking with a few sections of loose sand.

Vehicle campsites: Bobby Jo (two campsites), Horsehoof (one campsite), and New Bates Wilson Camp (two campsites).

Special attractions: Confluence Overlook and challenging sections for experienced four-wheelers.

Special precautions: The Confluence Overlook is unfenced, so please be careful, especially with kids.

Miles and Directions

0.5 South Boundary Hill (short rocky section).

3.8 Road to Bobby Jo and Horsehoof Camps.

4.7 Road to Chesler Park Trailhead.

5.0 Devils Pocket Trailhead.

6.6 SOB Hill.

7.8 Road to Devils Kitchen Camp, Lower Red Lake Trailhead.

8.4 Silver Stairs.

8.7 One-way road to Elephant Hill.

9.1 New Bates Wilson Camp.

11.4 Confluence Overlook foot trail.

12.0 Junction with roads to Confluence Overlook (west) and Cyclone Canyon Trail.

12.3 Confluence Overlook Trailhead.

Elephant Hill/ Devils Pocket Loop

Start: Elephant Hill Trailhead.

Finding the trailhead: From the entrance station, drive 3.1 miles on the main park road until you see a paved road going off to the left to Squaw Flat Campground and Elephant Hill. Take this left and then 0.3 mile later take a right onto another paved road. Take another right 0.5 mile later onto the unpaved, two-wheel-drive Elephant Hill Road. Once on the unpaved road, it's 3 miles to the trailhead. Drive slowly on this road, especially around several blind corners.

Distance: 9.4 miles.

Approximate time required: 5 to 7 hours.

Maps: Trails Illustrated Needles and USGS The Loop.

Permits: No permit required for day use. Permits required for vehicle camping or at-large backpacking.

Minimum vehicle requirements: High-clearance four-wheel-drive.

Difficulty: Difficult.

Road conditions: Starting right at the trailhead, Elephant Hill is extremely technical four-wheeling, as is the Silver Stairs section about halfway around the loop. Plus, there are a few more difficult sections. Between these rocky, technical spots, however, the road is easy driving on packed dirt with some loose sand. Keep in mind that this one-way loop can only be done in a clockwise direction.

Suitability for mountain biking: Fair to good with slow going in technical sections over Elephant Hill and Silver Stairs and through some short sections of loose sand.

Vehicle campsites: Devils Kitchen (four campsites), nestled amid large boulders and narrow spots between rock formations.

Special attractions: Definitely challenging for the experienced four-wheeler.

Special precautions: Be sure to check which sections of the loop are one-way travel only.

Miles and Directions

1.5 Junction with one-way road.

3.5 Devils Kitchen Camp, Devils Pocket Trailhead.

4.5 Junction with Devils Lane Road, Lower Red Lake Trailhead.

5.1 Silver Stairs.

6.1 Junction with one-way road.

8.3 Junction with Elephant Hill Road.

9.4 Elephant Hill Trailhead.

Canyonlands National Park: The Maze

The backcountry roads of the Maze should probably be viewed as trails that vehicles and mountain bikes use instead of as roads. The conditions are primitive, so you must be prepared—both mentally—and with a vehicle in excellent condition.

Horseshoe Canyon

Start: Hans Flat Ranger Station.

Distance: From Hans Flat, 22 miles (one-way) to the bottom of Horseshoe Canyon.

Approximate time required: To High Spur Camp, 1 hour; to canyon rim, 2 hours; to the bottom of canyon, 2.5 hours.

Maps: Trails Illustrated Maze District/Northeast Glen Canyon and USGS Head Spur and Sugarloaf Butte.

Permits: Permit required for vehicle camping at the High Spur campsite. Camping is not permitted in Horseshoe Canyon.

Minimum vehicle requirements: First 5 miles, low-clearance two-wheel-drive; to rim of canyon, high-clearance four-wheel-drive; to the bottom of canyon, high-clearance four-wheel-drive; on Deadman's Trail, high-clearance four-wheel-drive; on the side road to High Spur Camp, high-clearance four-wheel-drive.

Difficulty: Easy to canyon rim, extremely difficult into canyon.

Road conditions: Excellent the first 5 miles, then conditions worsen slightly. It's packed dirt and loose sand with a few short rocky sections all the way to rim of Horseshoe Canyon. The road down into the canyon is rocky, steep, narrow, and technical four-wheeling. Most people stop at the rim of canyon and walk the road into canyon. Grazing is allowed in Glen Canyon NRA, so watch for cattle on the road.

Suitability for mountain biking: Flat except for the drop into the canyon, easy going in most places with a few stretches of loose sand in first 10 miles and near the canyon rim. Side roads to High Spur Camp and up Deadman's Trail are also excellent for mountain biking.

Vehicle camps: High Spur Camp on east side of road 10 miles north of Hans Flat, 1 mile off main road and in the shadow of a huge sandstone formation, which rises abruptly out of the mesa. Get a great view of Cleopatra's

Chair, which really looks like a chair from here. Grazing is allowed in Glen Canyon NRA, so you could have a cow in camp.
Special attractions: Horseshoe Canyon.

Special precautions: Watch for cattle on the road. If you decide to drive into Horseshoe Canyon, go slowly and carefully.

Miles and Directions

10.0 Turnoff to High Spur Camp.

12.0 Leave Glen Canyon NRA.

12.6 Turnoff to Deadman's Trail.

20.0 Rim of Horseshoe Canyon.

22.0 Bottom of Horseshoe Canyon.

North Point

Start: Hans Flat Ranger Station.
Distance: From Gordon Flats Road, 7 miles (one-way) to where road splits to Cleopatra's Chair and Panorama Point.
Approximate time required: 1 hour (one-way).
Maps: Trails Illustrated Maze District/Northeast Glen Canyon and USGS Elaterite Basin and Cleopatra's Chair.
Permits: Vehicle camping or at-large backpacking permit required. Day use allowed with no permit.

Minimum vehicle requirements: High-clearance four-wheel-drive.
Difficulty: Moderate.
Road conditions: Mostly through juniper and piñon pines on the mesa. Several long, very steep, rocky sections intermingled with smooth sections of packed dirt. There is some loose sand with one mile-long smooth section through a big open park. Good scenery most of the way.
Suitability for mountain biking: Mostly excellent conditions—flat terrain, packed dirt with a few rocky sections and some loose sand.

Panorama Point

Start: End of North Point Road.
Distance: From end of North Point Road, 2 miles (one-way) to Panorama Point overlook and camp.
Approximate time required: 20 to 30 minutes (one-way).
Maps: Trails Illustrated Maze District/Northeast Glen Canyon and USGS Cleopatra's Chair.
Permits: Vehicle camping or at-large backpacking permit required. Day use allowed with no permit.

Minimum vehicle requirements: High-clearance four-wheel-drive.
Difficulty: Moderate.
Road conditions: Packed dirt with frequent rocky sections and ledges and a long stretch of solid slickrock near the end of the road. Truly spectacular scenery from Panorama Point.
Suitability for mountain biking: Excellent conditions.
Vehicle camps: Panorama Point is probably the most scenic campsite in the Maze—or

anywhere else! There's a great vista down into Elaterite Basin with the Maze in the distance to the east and Ekker Butte to the north and Elaterite Butte to the south. The camp is right at the end of the road in junipers and piñon pines and just a few feet from the edge of the cliff, so if you have children, watch them carefully. Panorama Point may be closed to camping in the spring due to nesting peregrine falcons, so be sure to check with a ranger before making your final plans.

Special attractions: World-famous view from end of road.

Special precautions: Extremely steep cliff at end of road and near camp. Very exposed and windy.

Cleopatra's Chair

Distance: From end of North Point Road, 3 miles (one-way) to end of road and Cleopatra's Chair Camp.

Approximate time required: 20 to 30 minutes (one-way).

Maps: Trails Illustrated Maze District/Northeast Glen Canyon and USGS Cleopatra's Chair.

Permits: Vehicle camping or at-large backpacking permit required. Day use allowed with no permit.

Camping below massive Cleopatra's Chair.

Minimum vehicle requirements: High-clearance four-wheel-drive.
Road conditions: Mostly packed dirt with a few short rocky sections.
Suitability for mountain biking: Excellent conditions.
Vehicle camps: Cleopatra's Chair Camp is at the end of the road in the south shadow of massive Cleopatra's Chair (which really doesn't look like a chair from this viewpoint) and about 100 feet from a great overlook into sprawling Millard Canyon.
Special precautions: Be extra cautious around the steep cliff at end of road and near camp.

Gordon Flats

Start: Hans Flat Ranger Station.
Distance: From Hans Flat Ranger Station, 12.1 miles (one-way) to where the road forks with left-hand fork going down the Flint Trail and the right-hand fork going to the Big Ridge.
Approximate time required: 1 hour (one-way).
Maps: Trails Illustrated Maze District/Northeast Glen Canyon and USGS Gordon Flats.
Permits: Vehicle camping or at-large backpacking permit required. Day use allowed without a permit.
Minimum vehicle requirements: Low-clearance two-wheel-drive.
Road conditions: One of the best roads in the Maze/Orange Cliffs area, mostly packed dirt. It can be driven with almost any vehicle.
Suitability for mountain biking: Excellent conditions.
Vehicle camps: Flint Seep Camp is only about 100 yards west of the Gordon Flats Road nestled in a grove of junipers and piñon pines. This camp has been established as a group site with a limit of sixteen people and five vehicles. Call the park reservation office to reserve this campsite.

Miles and Directions

2.2 French's Cabin.
2.4 French's Spring.
2.5 North Point Road.
9.1 Bagpipe Butte Overlook.
11.1 Flint Seep Camp.
11.9 Flint Trail Overlook.
12.1 Flint Trail/The Big Ridge Junction.

The Big Ridge

Start: Flint Trail junction.
Distance: 8 miles (one-way) from Flint Trail junction to Glen Canyon NRA boundary.
Approximate time required: 1 to 2 hours (one-way).
Maps: Trails Illustrated Maze District/Northeast Glen Canyon and USGS Gordon Flats and Clearwater Canyon.
Permits: Vehicle camping or at-large backpacking permit required. Day use allowed with no permit.

Minimum vehicle requirements: High-clearance two-wheel-drive.

Road conditions: More rocky than most roads in the area, but not extreme. Mostly flat as it stays on top of the Big Ridge Mesa. Gets worse after the Neck, even rockier and some bad gullies. Goes through juniper and piñon pines most of the way. About 3 miles past the park boundary (around the old Simplot Landing Strip), the road becomes impassable.

Suitability for mountain biking: Flat, mostly packed dirt, with minimal loose sand and frequent short rocky sections.

Vehicle camps: The Neck Camp is just off the west side of the road where the mesa narrows into a narrow "neck" like a similar spot in the Island in the Sky. Good scenery from the campsite. To get to Happy Canyon Camp, take the side road heading west off the main road about a mile past the Flint Trail junction and follow it for about 0.4 mile until you see the camp on your left. The road continues on for another 100 yards where it ends at the trailhead for the Happy Canyon Trail and a good view of the Henry Mountains to the south.

Miles and Directions (from Flint Trail/Gordon Flats junction):

0.9 Turn to Happy Canyon.

2.3 The Neck Camp.

8.0 Glen Canyon NRA Boundary.

The Flint Trail

Start: Gordon Flats Road.

Distance: From Gordon Flats Road, 2.8 miles (one-way) to Maze Overlook Road.

Approximate time required: 1 hour (one-way).

Maps: Trails Illustrated Maze District/Northeast Glen Canyon and USGS Clearwater Canyon and Teapot Rock.

Permits: Vehicle camping or at-large backpacking permit required. Day use allowed without a permit.

Minimum vehicle requirements: High-clearance four-wheel-drive with a short wheelbase is best for the tight turns on the switchbacks.

Road conditions: The first part of the road is a very steep series of switchbacks from The Big Ridge down the Orange Cliffs to another small mesa. When dry, the switchbacks are easily passable with extra attention from the driver. But when wet, the clay gets too slippery to drive. If you get caught in a rainstorm, wait until the clay dries out before attempting the Flint Trail.

Suitability for mountain biking: Good conditions when dry, but use extreme caution and keep the speed down when going down the switchbacks.

Special precautions: Go slowly on switchbacks and avoid them when wet. Chains are required for all four wheels in winter when snow is on the ground.

Maze Overlook

Start: Hans Flat Trailhead.
Distance: From Hans Flat, 27.5 miles (one-way) to the Maze Overlook Camps. From the junction with Flint Trail, 15.4 miles to the Maze Overlook Camps.
Approximate time required: From Hans Flat Ranger Station, 3 to 4 hours (one-way); from the Flint Trail junction, 2 to 3 hours (one-way).
Maps: Trails Illustrated Maze District/Northeast Glen Canyon and USGS Elaterite Basin and Teapot Rock.
Permits: Vehicle camping or at-large backpacking permit required. Day use allowed with no permit.
Minimum vehicle requirements: High-clearance four-wheel-drive.
Road conditions: Some sections are easy going, but most of the road is rocky (both loose rock and slickrock) with some steep sections and several ledges where clearance is critical. You'll want to get out of your vehicle to carefully check the route. Probably the toughest section is just past the Golden Stairs turnoff, as you drop off the mesa into Big Water Canyon. Great scenery all the way with the Orange Cliffs on the western horizon as you take a big turn around Elaterite Butte.

Suitability for mountain biking: Mostly good conditions with frequent rocky sections and minimal loose sand. Conditions turn to excellent after the junction with the Millard Canyon Road. Spectacular scenery all the way.
Vehicle camps: Both Maze Overlook 1 and Maze Overlook 2 are gorgeous campsites in the shadow of the fabulous Chocolate Drops towers, which are sculpted from Organ Rock shale. You can see it all from these camps: the Maze, Elaterite Butte, Ekker Butte, Panorama Point, the Land of Standing Rocks, and even the mighty La Sal Mountains serving as a backdrop to the east. The camps are quite exposed, however, so they can be unpleasant on a windy day. The camps also are extremely popular, so get your reservation in early.
Special attractions: Outstanding scenery along the road and from Maze Overlook Camps.

Miles and Directions (from Flint Trail junction):

2.6	Golden Stairs turnoff.
10.2	Millard Canyon junction.
11.8	Canyonlands National Park boundary.
15.4	Maze Overlook Camps, Trailhead and parking area.

Golden Stairs

Start: Maze Overlook Road.
Distance: From Maze Overlook Road, 1 mile (one-way) to Golden Stairs Camp and parking area.

Approximate time required: 20 to 30 minutes (one-way).
Maps: Trails Illustrated Maze District/Northeast Glen Canyon and USGS Elaterite Basin.

◀ *Camping below Standing Rock.*

Permits: Vehicle camping or at-large backpacking permit required. Day use allowed with no permit.

Minimum vehicle requirements: High-clearance four-wheel-drive.

Road conditions: Mostly rocky with ledges.

Suitability for mountain biking: Slightly rough mountain biking on this short side road from the Maze Overlook Road to Golden Stairs Camp.

Vehicle camps: Golden Stairs Camp sits up high on a 6,000-foot mesa crowned with junipers and piñon pines. The view right from camp is not great, but a short walk gives you superb vistas in several directions.

Millard Canyon

Start: Hans Flat Ranger Station.

Distance: From Hans Flat Ranger Station, 23.0 miles (one-way) to the Green River.

Approximate time required: From Hans Flat Ranger Station, 4 to 5 hours (one-way) to Millard Canyon Camp.

Maps: Trails Illustrated Maze District/Northeast Glen Canyon and USGS Turks Head, Cleopatra's Chair, and Horsethief Canyon.

Permits: Vehicle camping or at-large backpacking permit required. Day use allowed with no permit.

Minimum vehicle requirements: High-clearance four-wheel-drive.

Road condition: Conditions vary on this long stretch of road. Many sections are rocky and slow going, but nothing extreme. Just before you reach Millard Canyon Camp and the Green River, the road gets very rocky.

Suitability for mountain biking: Good to excellent conditions most of the way with a few rocky sections, especially near the end where road heads down to the river.

Vehicle camps: Ekker Butte is not one of the prime campsites in the area. It's mostly slickrock, and tent camping is marginal. The NPS considers it an overflow site, so it's usually available. The Millard Canyon Camp is right on the Green River and is one of the nicest campsites in the Maze.

Special attractions: Great campsite on the Green River, and you probably will have the area to yourself.

Miles and Directions (from the turnoff to the Maze Overlook):

0.3 North Trail Trailhead.

2.0 Canyonlands National Park boundary (no sign).

9.2 Ekker Butte Camp.

23.0 Millard Canyon Camp.

Sunset Pass

Start: Waterhole Flat junction.

Distance: From Waterhole Flat junction, 4.5 miles (one-way) to Glen Canyon NRA boundary.

Approximate time required: From Waterhole Flat junction, 1 to 2 hours (one-way) to Glen Canyon NRA boundary.

Maps: Trails Illustrated Maze District/Northeast Glen Canyon and USGS Clearwater Canyon.

Permits: Vehicle camping or at-large backpacking permit required. Day use allowed without a permit.

Minimum vehicle requirements: High-clearance four-wheel-drive.

Road conditions: Packed dirt most of the way with a few short rocky sections and one long section just on the east side of the pass, which is actually a gap in the Orange Cliffs.

Suitability for mountain biking: Excellent conditions with a moderately steep climb to the pass.

Vehicle camps: Sunset Pass Camp is in a grove of junipers and piñyon pines on the south side of the road just as it goes through the gap in the Orange Cliffs. It's exposed to the wind and rain, but not nearly as much as popular campsites such as Maze Overlook or Standing Rock.

Miles and Directions (from Waterhole Flat Junction):

2.5 Sunset Pass Camp.

4.5 Glen Canyon NRA boundary.

Waterhole Flat

Start: Flint Trail junction.

Distance: 6.5 miles (one-way) to Waterhole Flat junction.

Approximate time required: From Flint Trail junction, 1 hour (one-way).

Maps: Trails Illustrated Maze District/Northeast Glen Canyon and USGS Clearwater Canyon and Teapot Rock.

Permits: Vehicle camping or at-large backpacking permit required. Day use allowed with no permit.

Minimum vehicle requirements: High-clearance two-wheel-drive from Hite; high-clearance four-wheel-drive from Hans Flat Ranger Station.

Road conditions: From the Flint Trail junction to the Waterhole Flat junction, it's packed dirt with a few short rocky sections but easy going all the way, especially the southernmost half of this section of road where it gets so good that you might have to be careful not to exceed the 15 mph speed limit. The north half goes between precipitous Red Cove on the east and massive Orange Cliffs on the west, both well-named for their color, and the south half goes across the broad, mostly flat terrain of Waterhole Flat. On some older maps, you may see a road heading west over to Sunset Pass, but that road has been recently abandoned. The same old map might show a road heading south down a wash to Dollhouse Road. This looks like a shortcut, but it isn't an official road and probably takes longer than driving the long way around. The long route is easy driving, and you can make great time compared to driving through the narrow, rocky wash.

Suitability for mountain biking: Excellent road for mountain biking.

The Road to the Dollhouse

Start: Waterhole Flat junction.

Distance: 21 miles (one-way).

Approximate time required: From Waterhole Flat junction, 3 to 4 hours (one-way) to the Dollhouse.

Maps: Trails Illustrated Maze District/Northeast Glen Canyon and USGS Teapot Rock, Elaterite Basin and Spanish Bottom.

Permits: Vehicle camping or at-large backpacking permit required. Day use allowed without a permit.

Minimum vehicle requirements: High-clearance four-wheel-drive.

Road conditions: From the Waterhole Flat junction, the road starts out smooth and stays that way for about 3 miles. Then it gradually gets rougher as you approach the Teapot Rock Camp. After passing by the campsite, you face a 5-mile section of road that is probably the worst in the Maze District, and you probably can walk it faster than you can drive it. You must get out of your vehicle frequently to check routes over ledges and in rocky sections. Use extreme caution all the way unless you want to seriously damage your vehicle and get stranded in the Maze. After you reach the Wall Camp, the road gets better, turning into mostly packed sand with a few rocky sections. From Chimney Rock to the Dollhouse, the road has sections of loose sand and gets seriously rocky just before the Dollhouse.

Suitability for mountain biking: Conditions may be better for mountain biking than they are for driving, especially in the section from Teapot Rock Camp to the Wall Camp. After the Chimney Rock Camp, the road has some sections of loose sand. Some loose sand and rocky sections may prove difficult for novice riders, but for the most part, this is a fantastic mountain biking road.

Vehicle camps: Vehicle camps in the Maze do not have vault toilets. You are required to have a portable toilet with you.

Teapot Rock Camp—The road goes right by this camp, so privacy can be a problem. Plus it's very rocky and exposed, but it does have a great view of Teapot Rock. Also, if you don't have a high-clearance four-wheel-drive vehicle, you can camp here and hike or mountain bike into the Maze area.

The Wall Camp—On the north side of the road about 100 yards off the road. Very scenic campsite with great view of the Maze, Chocolate Drops, Standing Rock and many other famous formations. Very exposed, so it can be unpleasant on a windy day.

Standing Rock—Right in the shadow of awesome Standing Rock, so you can sit in camp for hours and wonder how this smokestack-like sandstone spire survived the power of nature. Like the Wall Camp, this camp is about 100 yards north of the road and is quite exposed.

Chimney Rock—Following the trend set by the Wall and Standing Rock, this camp is just north of the road and very exposed, but has incredible scenery. It has the attraction of being right by a major trailhead for trails and off-trail routes into the Maze and serves as a base camp for hikers who like day hiking instead of backpacking.

Dollhouse 1—Semi-protected between two massive sandstone towers, but still with a good view off to the east. Close to the trailheads for designated trails leaving the Dollhouse area. This camp, along with the other two Dollhouse camps, has the advantage of privacy, since all these are located at the end of spur roads.

Dollhouse 2—Like Camp 1, Camp 2 is tucked amid the Dollhouse towers. More exposed than Camp 1, which can be a

The Dollhouse.

problem on windier days, but less exposed than Camp 3.

Dollhouse 3—Unlike Camp 1 and 2, you can get a great view of the Dollhouse itself from Camp 3. It's in an open area on the southwest edge of the famous sandstone formation. This can be the least desirable of the three on a windy day, but the most desirable in good weather. Also, Camp 3 is farther from the official trailheads for the three designated trails leaving the Dollhouse area.

Special attractions: Truly spectacular scenery and the aura of remoteness and self-reliance.

Special precautions: Hazardous road.

Miles and Directions (from Waterhole Flat junction):

- **3.6** Teapot Rock Camp.
- **9.2** Golden Stairs Trailhead.
- **10.3** Canyonlands National Park boundary.
- **13.8** The Wall Camp.
- **15.8** Standing Rock Camp.
- **17.1** Chimney Rock Camp.
- **17.2** Harvest Scene Trailhead.

20.6 Turn to Dollhouse 3 Camp.

20.7 Colorado/Green River Overlook Trailhead.

20.8 Spanish Bottom and Granary Trailhead.

21.0 Dollhouse 1 and 2 Camps.

Hite

Start: Waterhole Flat junction.
Distance: 32 miles (one-way) to Hite.
Approximate time required: 2 to 3 hours (one-way) to Hite.
Maps: Trails Illustrated Maze District/Northeast Glen Canyon and USGS Clearwater Canyon and Bowdie Canyon West.
Minimum vehicle requirements: High-clearance two-wheel-drive.

Road conditions: With the exception of a few rocky sections near the Waterhole Flat junction, this is a two-wheel-drive road all the way to the paved road just before Hite.
Suitability for mountain biking: Excellent conditions for mountain biking, but not quite as scenic as many other roads in the Maze.

About the Author

Bill Schneider has spent thirty-five years hiking trails all across America. During college in the mid-1960s, he worked on a trail crew in Glacier National Park and became a hiking addict. He spent the 1970s publishing *Montana Outdoors* magazine for the Montana Department of Fish, Wildlife & Parks while covering as many miles of trails as possible on weekends and holidays. In 1979, Bill and his partner, Mike Sample, founded Falcon Publishing.

Since then, Bill has written twenty books and many magazine articles on wildlife, outdoor recreation, and environmental issues. Bill has also taught classes on bicycling, backpacking, zero-impact camping, and hiking in bear country for the Yellowstone Institute, a nonprofit educational organization in Yellowstone National Park.

In 2000 Bill retired from his position as president of Falcon Publishing (now part of The Globe Pequot Press) after it had grown into the premier publisher of outdoor recreation guidebooks with more than 700 titles in print. He now lives in Helena, Montana, with his wife, Marnie, and works as a publishing consultant and freelance writer.

Books by Bill Schneider

Learn more about Bill Schneider's other books at www.billschneider.net.

The Dakota Image, 1980

The Yellowstone River, 1985

Best Hikes on the Continental Divide, 1988

The Flight of the Nez Perce, 1988

The Tree Giants, 1988

Backpacking Tips, co-author, 2005

Best Backpacking Vacations Northern Rockies, 2002

Best Easy Day Hikes Yellowstone, 2003

Hiking Yellowstone National Park, 2003

Best Easy Day Hikes Absaroka-Beartooth Wilderness, 2003

Hiking the Absaroka-Beartooth Wilderness, 2003

Where the Grizzly Walks, 2003

Bear Aware: A Quick Reference Bear Country Survival Guide, 2004

Hiking Montana, co-author, 2004

Hiking Carlsbad Caverns & Guadalupe Mountains National Parks, 2005

Best Easy Day Hikes Grand Teton, 2005

Hiking Grand Teton National Park, 2005

Hiking Utah, 2005

Best Easy Day Hikes Canyonlands & Arches, 2005

WHAT'S SO SPECIAL ABOUT UNSPOILED, NATURAL PLACES?

Beauty   Solitude   Wildness   Freedom   Quiet   Adventure
Serenity   Inspiration   Wonder   Excitement
Relaxation   Challenge

There's a lot to love about our treasured public lands, and the reasons are different for each of us. Whatever your reasons are, the national **Leave No Trace** education program will help you discover special outdoor places, enjoy them, and preserve them—today and for those who follow. By practicing and passing along these simple principles, you can help protect the special places you love from being loved to death.

THE PRINCIPLES OF **LEAVE NO TRACE**

- Plan ahead and prepare
- Travel and camp on durable surfaces
- Dispose of waste properly
- Leave what you find
- Minimize campfire impacts
- Respect wildlife
- Be considerate of other visitors

Leave No Trace is a national nonprofit organization dedicated to teaching responsible outdoor recreation skills and ethics to everyone who enjoys spending time outdoors.

To learn more or to become a member, please visit us at www.LNT.org or call (800) 332-4100.

Leave No Trace, P.O. Box 997, Boulder, CO 80306